PORLOCK
IN THOSE DAYS

View of Porlock, c1950.

The High Street looking westwards (and deserted!) showing the Castle Hotel, built in 1890. The white building on the right was a farm, Higher Bourne, demolished and rebuilt as a row of shops and flats c1910.

The Dovery end of the village. The house on the left with the tall chimney is now Tesco's and the Café and Bicycle Hire. The house beyond it was burnt down in 1928.

PORLOCK
IN THOSE DAYS

Dennis Corner

RARE BOOKS AND BERRY

This revised edition first published in 2009 by

Rare Books and Berry
High Street, Porlock,
Minehead, Somerset
TA24 8PU

www.rarebooksandberry.co.uk

First Published in 1992
Exmoor Books

© Dennis Corner

A CIP catalogue record for this title is
Available from the British Library

ISBN 978-0-9557119-7-8

Designed and typeset in Minion at
Alacrity, Sandford, Somerset

Printed and bound by
Cromwell Press Group, Trowbridge, Wiltshire

CONTENTS

PORLOCK BAY

View of the bay and flooded marsh, due to a breach in the pebble ridge.
The marsh has now become a salt marsh.

HIGH-WATER in Porlock Bay. The tide upon the turn. Sand-pipers, great and small, dipping, nodding, stalking to and fro, or flitting along its margin waiting for the ebb; a gull riding smoothly outside on an untroubled surface, calm as the soft sky overhead, that smiled lovingly down on the Severn Sea. Landward, a strip of green and level meadows, fringed by luxuriant woodlands, fair with the gorgeous hues of summer; stalwart oak, towering elm, spreading walnut, stately Spanish chestnut, hard mountain ash, and scattered high on the steep, above dotted thorns and spreading hazels, outposts, as it were, of delicate feathering birches, to guard the borders of the forest and the waste; fairyland brought here to upper earth, with all its changing phases, and variety of splendour.

G.J. Whyte-Melville, from *Katerfelto*, 1875

INTRODUCTION

I WAS BORN in Somerset, namely at Worle, which was a small village outside Weston-super-Mare at that time and now is a great sprawling place of housing estates. I lived there until, at the age of six, I moved with my mother to live with her parents at Porlock, my father having died. Porlock had been the family home of my mother's people for generations, so I think I am practically a native of the place.

My boyhood days with other lads of the village were wonderful days, especially as we just roamed the countryside looking at the wildlife, which was more plentiful and varied then

The local farmers were very tolerant and didn't object to us walking in their fields, but we did know not to walk in crops or in a field which was let up for hay, and we didn't break down gates or hedges. Often in our escapades, I and others fell in the rivers or the sea, or the marsh. I think for several years I had perpetual wet feet.

This and the life at school, clubs, Scouts and so on, gave me a great love of Porlock and its beautiful surroundings. Later in my working days, and in the village organisations, I met and talked with so many interesting people that I began to make note of what they told me, and this, together with reading about the area and visiting many places around, and walking many miles over the moor and environs, gave me the idea of this book about the people and places that have fascinated me.

I hope that the reader will find it interesting.

High Street, c1950.

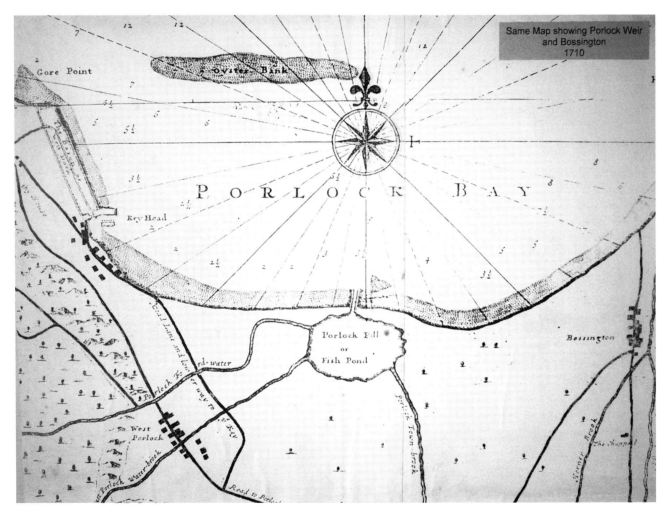

Map of Porlock Bay, prepared in the period 1710-20. Note the oyster bed in the bay and the old way to Porlock Weir.

8

1

SOME NOTES ON PORLOCK

PORLOCK IN WEST SOMERSET is an ancient village situated in a very sheltered valley, open to the Bristol Channel, six miles west of Minehead. Its name is believed to be of Saxon origin, meaning the locked port, which would indicate that it always had trade by the sea. Some historians believe that there was at one time a harbour at what is now Porlock Marsh. One piece of evidence for this is the absence of any mention of Porlock Weir, or the present harbour, in any records before the fifteenth century. Another is the fact that Sparkhayes Lane, which runs down to the beach from near the centre of the village, is a very deep lane, which may indicate that it was extensively used for transporting goods up from the port. However, it could also have been dug out as a boundary, many early boundaries being quite deep ditches with a hedge a-top. Again, it could originally have been the bed of a stream.

The earliest map of Porlock Manor, dated 1710, shows Porlock Marsh as a large pill or fish pond with an outlet to the sea. 'Pill', meaning a tidal creek or harbour, is a term well known in the Bristol Channel area, being used at Pilton in Barnstaple, Uphill, Newport, and of course Pill on the Avon below Bristol. An outlet to the sea is seen on the map – later an outlet with a sluice gate, which closed against the incoming tide and opened as the tide ebbed. Known as the 'New Works', this was built in 1910 as a big drainage

Morning view from Hurlestone Point.
Note the ridges left by the tides.

scheme in order to drain the marsh. Later attempts to drain the marsh have been made, notably by the Somerset River Board in the 1960s, although the Chief Engineer said at the time that they would never drain it completely. The high tides are higher than the land behind the pebble ridge and the sea just percolates through the pebbles, or occasionally comes over the top of the beach. The pebble ridge, a remarkable natural phenomenon, stretches from Hurlstone Point

The water draining back from the marsh through the gap, creating a deep drop which can be dangerous to cross.

to Gore Point; west of Porlock Weir it forms a semi-circle which is Porlock Bay, protecting the land.

The coast must have changed at various stages, and even during this last century there are regular reports of landslips at Porlockford and in the Culbone Woods. At Porlockford and Porlock Weir a sea wall was built and has had to be extended. At low water, at Redsands, opposite West Porlock, there are still the remains of a submarine forest, which, it is believed, was woodland thousands of years ago. Imagine the whole vale being a swampy woodland; the vale we know today, with its patchwork of fields, has gradually been tamed over many centuries. Since 1990 the sea has risen and the marsh has now become a salt marsh: 70 per cent of the tides enter through the gap left in the beach, resulting in trees, bushes and reeds being killed and plants tolerant to salt water taking their place. Maybe in time the sea will recede again, and the pebble ridge be restored.

The Horner Water reaches the beach at Bossington, where it normally fills up a large pond known as the Avon Pool. The water seeps through the pebbles to the sea. On some occasions when there is a very high river, after continuous heavy rain, the amount of water is so great that the pond fills up and water floods back towards Bossington, forming a huge lake. The pressure becomes so great that eventually the water pushes the stones away, and with a mighty rush it makes its outlet to the sea, forming a channel through the ridge, often twenty or so feet deep. The outlet is filled up again as the high tides bring in pebbles once more.

From Hurlstone Point there is a good view of the pebble ridge and the lines where the various tides have left their mark are clear to see. It is amazing to think that many of those rounded pebbles near the point started out as rocks from the cliffs down channel, as far away as Ilfracombe. The beach is somewhat like the Chesil Beach at Portland. An old map of Bossington Farm names the field near Bossington Lime Kiln as 'Chesil'.

Referring again to the map of 1710, there is shown a lower road to Porlock Weir which left the present road just before West Porlock and followed the Court Lease Lane (Cow Lane) to cross the stream below Porlockford and follow through beside the beach to Porlock Weir. The other road to the weir is the present Top Road. The Lower Road, as we know it, was not built until the later 1800s.

2

EARLY TIMES IN PORLOCK

ANCIENT MAN LIVED, hunted and later farmed on Exmoor. Various earthworks, camps or castles can be seen around the district. The nearest are Bury Castle, Selworthy, Berry Castle, at the top of Hawkcombe, and Sweetworthy, above Cloutsham. There are also many burial mounds; although several have disappeared, there are still some in the Dunkery area, and on Culbone Hill. The best known is at Alderman's Barrow. A stone row, and a stone with a wheeled cross on it believed to be 6th century, can also be seen on Culbone Hill, and there is a stone circle at Colly Water.

The most prominent and probably best known of the stones are the Whitstones, which lie between the junction of the A39 and the Exford Road. They were most likely a well-known landmark for people passing this way to Barnstaple. Legend has it that these stones were thrown from Hurlstone Point by the Devil and St Peter, or even St Dubricius, in contest with each other. Other traces of ancient man have been found. I have seen worked arrow heads from a field above Selworthy, as well as chippings of flint from Hawkcombe Head.

In Taunton Museum are the most ancient human remains found on Exmoor. The skeleton was discovered in 1896 by a man digging out stones for road repairs from the quarry on the A39, beyond the Broom Street Farm entrance. He had been buried in a *cyst* or *kystvain*, which is a form of coffin made of stone slabs. With him was buried a pot or beaker with a decorated edge. From this, archeologists were able to date the tomb to around c1500 BC. Other similar burials have been found. These early people, or 'beaker' folk as they were known, arrived in Britain from Western Europe some 2000 years BC. The beaker would have been buried so that the deceased could have a drink on his way to the next world. Ancient people really did believe that the dead were able to take grave goods with them to the next world. Sometimes a joint of meat and a dagger would be buried with them.

Later on the Celtic people lived in Porlock, but little trace of them can be found, except perhaps in a few place names and words in common use in West Somerset and North Devon. An example is the word *coombe* for a valley, which is similar to the Welsh *cwm*, the Welsh being descendents of the Celts. Another is *myne*, as in the farm names East Myne and West Myne on North Hill, and both Minehead and Dunkery are believed to be Celtic names.

The Saxons came next and gradually took over Southern England; they really began to farm the area. Porlock gets its name from the Saxon *Portloc*, or locked port, but we do not know by what name it was known earlier, or even if there was a settlement here before Saxon times.

We must not forget, however, that the Romans were in England for about three hundred years. Their activities do not appear to have been great in Porlock, although they had fine cities at Bath and Exeter. All we have is the still visible Roman Fort (Old Barrow) on the hill near the A39, above Glenthorne. It is believed that a garrison of about eighty soldiers, with a centurion, occupied this site for a few years before abandoning it for another fortlet at Martinhoe. These forts would have been used for watching the Channel, particularly for keeping an eye on the Silures, the tribe which the Romans failed to subdue on the Welsh side. Roman ships used the Channel, and the Romans had their port at Sea Mills, at the mouth of the Avon, near what is now Bristol. They may also have shipped lead, mined in the Mendip Hills, from the River Axe at Uphill. Tradition also speaks of Roman iron mines in the Brendon Hills and on Exmoor.

Regarding names, we can only wonder whether nearby Broomstreet derives its name from the Roman word *street*, and perhaps Stratford near Selworthy also.

That the area was thinly populated is confirmed by the Doomsday Survey taken twenty years after the Norman Conquest of 1066. For example, Porlock had only six villeins, three bordiers and six bondmen. If these represented heads of families, then, even with large families, there would have been less than two hundred people, perhaps nearer one hundred. Yet Porlock suffered two attacks or invasions, though in neither case were the inhabitants left to defend themselves, the attacks being directed against Somerset generally rather than Porlock in particular. The position of the place favoured the invader. The bay is well sheltered and, although the coast has undergone many changes (at one time the sea encroached considerably) the flat alluvual land was apparently a shallow and muddy inlet.

The *Anglo-Saxon Chronicle*, begun in about 890, gives a year-by-year account of national and regional events, as seen from the West Saxon point of view. Contemporary descriptions of Alfred's wars with the Danes are amongst the fullest entries.

In the year 918 a Danish expedition started from the coast of Armorica (Brittany). Edward, the son of Alfred the Great, was King, and he was ready for the emergency. Fortresses had been built in various parts, which helped to prevent the success of the Danish expedition. After ravaging the coast of Wales, the Danish pirates attempted to penetrate into Herefordshire. Opposed by the inhabitants, supported by neighbouring strongholds, they suffered defeat. Driven into a wood, they were compelled to give hostages as security to guarantee that they would leave England unmolested in the future. But Edward was doubtful of their honour, and with the prudence of a far-seeing general lined the coast of Somerset with troops. The Danes made two more attempts to land, one at Watchet and one at Porlock, but they were defeated in both places, with great loss. Two of their leaders, Earl Harold and the brother of Earl Otter, were slain. The survivors fled to the island of Flat Holm, then uninhabited, but want compelled them to abandon their place of refuge and seek better fortune in Ireland. We know from excavations in Dublin that there was a Danish settlement there.

Perhaps the descendants of these Danes took part in another and more formidable attack on Porlock about 130 years later, in the time of Edward the Confessor. Aelfgar, the son of Leofric the great Earl of Mercia, was Lord of the Manor of Porlock, as of many other manors in Somerset and Devon. There was rivalry and hatred between this family and that of the Earl Godwine. In 1051 Godwine and his sons had been declared outlaws. Godwine fled to Flanders to await the course of events, but his two sons, Harold (afterwards King) and Leofivine were impatient. They went to Ireland, where many towns were peopled by Danish settlers, and raised a small army. With nine ships they sailed into Porlock Bay in 1052. They landed at a spot between Porlock and Porlock Weir; there is a field which goes by the name of Hellbyes, near Porlockford, where, during the last century, fragments of weapons were found. Numbers flocked to resist the invasion, but Harold and his well-drilled body of men, with nothing before them but to do or die, succeeded in reaching Porlock. They burnt every building and carried off what spoil they could. Thirty theyns and a great number of other people were slain that day.

Collinson, who wrote a history of Somerset in about 1750, says that even then men of Porlock used to point

An ancient British tomb discovered beside the A39 by a roadman taking out stone from the quarry beyond the Broomstreet Farm entrance in 1896.

out the remains of buildings which had been burnt, as they supposed, at the great foray of Harold. It has been suggested that Berry Castle in Hawkcombe was dug as a place of refuge either from the Danes or from the invasions of Harold, though it is more likely a hill fort of the Iron Age. It is now covered by trees, but originally would have been more open. The utter destruction of Porlock at that time would indicate that no part of the Church is dated earlier than 1051, although a piece of a Saxon cross, found at a much later date, can be seen there. It is believed to be the oldest worked stone in any church in the district.

From the Doomsday Survey we learn that the Lord of the Manor of Porlock before the Conquest was Aelgar. He is identified as the son of Leofric, Earl of Mercia.

On the coming of the Conqueror, the lands were conferred upon Baldwin, Bishop of Exeter as overlord. His underlord as tenant was Drogo, or, as he is called in the Exeter Doomsday, Rogo, son of Nigel. There seems to be little reason to doubt that he was of the Roges family which held the Manor down to the time of Edward III.

The Roges family were the Lords of Porlock for several generations, many of them bearing the name Simon. There used to be a meadow in Villes Lane, where it joined Furzeland Road, called Simon's Meade, now built on. The name implies that it had been the property of Simon Roges.

Later the Manor was held by Sir Nigel Loring, who, in the year 1366, was granted a Market to be held on Thursday every week, and also three Fairs to be held annually within the Manor, each lasting three days. By the same charter Sir Nigel had leave to impark his woods at Porlock to preserve the game. To the present day the woods to the west of Porlock are known as the Parks. There is a deep ditch and bank which marks the boundary at the top of Higher Park, above the Toll Road. It was probably dug at the time the Park was made.

Visiting Porlock today, entering the High Street from the Minehead direction, we descend Dunster Steep, probably so named because it was the main road out to Dunster. Because of the Castle and the Port of Dunster, Dunster was more important than Minehead before the Minehead harbour was built by the Luttrels of Dunster Castle. The present way down into Porlock is the old steep, the original way. Dunster Steep was in the part of Porlock known as Dovery or Doverhay, belonging, prior to 1930, to the Parish of Luccombe. The Dovery part of Luccombe stretched as far as the beach in a long arm known as the Luccombe Corridor.

It included a thousand feet of beach, no doubt to give Luccombe its own access to the sea, possibly for fishing.

Dovery is mentioned in the Doomsday Survey of 1086, which states: 'Roger has a Manor called Doveri which Edema held TRE [in the reign of Edward] and rendered geld for 1 Virgate. One team can plough it. Alric holds it of Roger, Alric has there 2 Villeins and 1 Bordier, and it is worth 7 shillings and 6 pence. When Roger received it, it was worth 10 shillings.'

The Doomsday description of Porlock is thus: 'Baldwin has a Manor called Portloc, which Algar held TRE and rendered geld for 3 hides. 12 teams can plough it. Roger, son of Nigel holds it of Baldwin, and has 1 hide and a half in demesne and the Villeins have the other lands. Rogo has there 6 Villeins, 3 Bordiers, 6 Serfs, 300 acres of wood and 500 acres of pasture. It is worth 25 shillings, when Baldwin received it, it was worth 4 pounds.'

It is clear that Porlock was much bigger than Dovery. The two places were divided by a stream which still runs from the main Hawkcombe Stream to the Recreation Ground, through the Rectory land and under the Drang into Tinker's Orchard, passing between Rawles Buildings and Lowerbourne. It then runs under the main street near the hairdresser's shop and finally back into the Hawkcombe Stream again. The old boundary was the main street from the hairdresser's until it met another stream which passes under the road near the entrance to England's Road.

This meant that those people who lived in Lowerbourne, for example, or Bond's and Marley's Rows, belonged to the Parish of Luccombe, as can be witnessed by the names of some of the Dovery people on the War Memorial Roll of Honour in Luccombe Church. As children they would have been taken to church at Luccombe, where their allegiance was. As late as 1928 a petition was organised by residents of Dovery asking that they remain in the Parish of Luccombe, as there was a proposal to bring Dovery into Porlock.

3

THE CHURCH OF ST DUBRICIUS

View of the village, c1885, showing the houses in Parson Street.

MUCH HAS BEEN WRITTEN about the Church, and various guides have been published. However, there are many articles of interest in the Church, and things to be said about its foundation.

The Church is dedicated to St Dubricius, or St Deveroe as he used to be called. The Welsh knew him as Dyfrig. He is believed to have been born about AD 450 in Madley, six miles west of Hereford. A lot is

The restoration of the Parish Church in the 1880s. It was reopened by the Lord Bishop of the diocese on 28th May 1891. Note the houses around the church being demolished.

Brendan, the great Irish missionary and voyager (who, it now seems fairly certain, sailed as far as America), at Brendon; St Petroc at Timberscombe, West Anstey and Parracombe; St Decuman at Watchet; St Carantoc at Carhampton; St Beuno at Culbone, and so on.

The cross-legged effigy in the arched recess in the south aisle is of a 15th-century knight in chain armour traditionally said to represent a member of the Roges

The Church after restoration. The church clock was installed at the time of Queen Victoria's Diamond Jubilee in 1897.

known about his activities in Herefordshire from a record of land grants made to him by the reigning kings in order to found *llans* (churches). As a bishop he was wise, and a great teacher. He is co-patron of Llandaff Cathedral and patron of several churches in Herefordshire. There is a chapel dedicated to him in Llandaff. It is mainly due to Dubricius that Hereford embraced and fostered the Christian faith a century before St Augustine came to Canterbury as a missionary from St Gregory the Great to the inhabitants of Kent in AD 597. Dubricius is said to have crowned King Arthur, and married him to Queen Guinevere, but this is only one of the legends of Glastonbury. Dubricius lived to a great age, spending his later years as a hermit on Bardsey Island off the Llyn Peninsula in West Wales. He died c546. A stained glass window in memory of the Rev Walter Hook, which is in the tower, depicts St Dubricius. Whether he ever visited Porlock is not known, but what may be regarded as certain is that the first Church in Porlock was founded by St Dubricius or someone in close association with him.

Other dedications of churches in this area are of Celtic saints, perhaps better described as holy men, who came from Wales and Ireland: St

The Harrington Memorial in St Dubricius Church.

or, as they were known, the FitzRoges family. It is believed that the FitzRoges were the builders of the present Church.

About the middle of the 14th century the Manor passed to Sir Nigel Loring, a distinguished soldier and devout churchman. At his death his estates were divided between his two daughters. Porlock fell to Isabella, who married Sir Robert Harrington of Aldingham in Lancashire. She died in 1400, and he in 1406. Their son Sir John, the 4th Baron, married Elizabeth, daughter of Edward Courtenay, 3rd Earl of Devon. Sir John went off to the French Wars in 1417-18, as a close follower of King Henry V. With him went a company of 86 archers and 29 lancers, men recruited from the Porlock district. Sir John failed to return; we do not know how he died. He left a long will with many bequests, which included the setting up of a Chantry. This was common practice amongst the nobility in those times. Two priests were to be employed to help with the work and services of the Church. They would celebrate Divine Service and pray for the souls of Lord and Lady Harrington's parents and ancestors.

It is believed that Chantry Cottage (formerly two cottages) in the Drang near the Church was where they lived. The cottages were prepared for them, and are believed to have been built before the Chantry bequest was carried out. This is thought to be the oldest dwelling in Porlock.

Although Sir John Harrington died in 1417, the Chantry was not set up for another fifty years. Lady Elizabeth had re-married. Her second husband, Sir William Bonville of Chewton Mendip, was beheaded by the Lancastrians after the battle of St Albans in 1461. Lady Elizabeth lived and spent much of her time at her Manors of Porlock and Brendon until her death in 1471.

The monument to her and her first husband is the finest carving in the Church, and in fact is said to be the finest of its kind in England. The knight is in plate armour of the period, the lady in a beautiful dress and headdress, also of the period. The monument and canopy was once richly coloured, but the natural dyes have almost completely faded away. The effigies are of alabaster, believed to have come from Chellaston, near Derby. In order to set up this Chantry and monument, the estate of Ugborough, near Plymouth was sold.

At the altar of the Church, on the tryptych can be seen:

Reredos in St Dubricius Church.

A 1 Arms of the Diocese of Bath and Wells above
       and of the County of Somerset below
    2 St Brendan, the great Irish missionary
    3 St Olave, Patron of the Chapel at Porlock Weir
    4 The Resurrection of our Lord
    5 St Bridget, the great Irish saint
    6 Adam Bellenden, Bishop of Aberdeen, Chancellor of
       the University, Rector of Porlock 1642-7
    7 The Arms of Bellenden above
       and of Kings College, Aberdeen below

B The reredos proper:
    1 St Dubricius or Dyfrig
    2 St Petroc
    3 The Crucifixion
    4 St Carontoc
    5 St George, Patron of England (and of Dunster,
       the principle church in the district)

C Shields of arms (reading from left to right):
    1 Courtenay
    2 Loring
    3 Harrington
    4 Bonville
    5 Fitz Roges
    6 Grey

The shields of arms were all those of families connected with the Manor of Porlock. After the death of Lady Harrington, the estate passed to the Grey family via Cecily Bonville, who was Baroness Bonville and Harrington in her own right and one of the richest women in England. Cecily Bonville, at sixteen years of age, had married Sir Thomas Grey, first Marquis of Dorset. The estate stayed in this family until the beheading of Lady Jane Grey, who had been proclaimed Queen of England on 6th July 1553 but reigned for only nine days.

Another item of interest in the Church is the ancient clock near the tower. It is one of the oldest in England. It was not taken down from the tower until the Diamond Jubilee of Queen Victoria, when the present clock was installed. It had neither face nor hands; it merely struck the hour on the tenor bell. There wasn't so much concern with time then; people didn't need to be on time for buses or trains. As everything was so much quieter, and the pace of life slower, men working in the fields or workshops would have heard the bell strike the hour. The clock is believed to date from the 1400s. In the Bailiff's accounts of the Manor of Brendon, is the entry: '…for the expenses of the Bailiff in riding from Brendon to Barnstaple and returning to Porlock for Roger the Clockmaker to fetch him to the Lady: 3d.' From this we gather that there must have been a clockmaker at Barnstaple who was at work in Porlock at that time. It is very likely that he made the clock, with Lady Harrington meeting the cost.

In the Church porch is a board commemorating Henry Rogers of Cannington. The Rogers family (not to be confused with the Roges) were Lords of the Manors of Cannington, Burnham and Porlock in the 17th century, to be followed by the Blathwayt family. It was this Henry Rogers who gave Porlock two of its charities, the Rogers

Charity and the Winsford Land Charity, which on 1st March 2009 were merged into one charity named the Henry Rogers Charities.

The most notable feature of Porlock Church from the outside is its truncated spire or steeple. No one knows for certain, but it is said to have been blown off in a gale in about 1700. Perhaps this was the great gale of 1703 which did great damage in Somerset, Wales and Monmouthshire. Then the spire was finished off in its present form. An amusing story is told. When the steeple was being built, the staghounds passed through the village. Being keen on hunting, the men downed tools and followed the hunt, and they didn't come back to finish the job. Another suggestion is that a light could be put on the top of the steeple to guide fishermen who were often fishing well into the night, in the days when herring fishing was so important. Whatever the reason, we do know that any church can have a pointed spire, but Porlock's blunt spire is unique.

Amongst the tombstones with many local names of families who have lived for generations in Porlock is one of special interest by the west corner of the tower. It is a pathetic epitaph on Thomas and Prudence Rawle, who died within a day of each other. It reads:

> He first departed; she for one
> day tried to live without
> Him, liked it not and dy'd.

Until the Second World War, the death bell or passing bell was rung (for a fee) on the death of a parishioner (during the war the bells were silenced, to be used only in the event of invasion or an air raid). This custom dates back to before the Reformation, Somerset and Devon being the last counties to keep it up. Another old custom was to rope the bride and groom: village children would hold a rope, with a horse shoe in the middle, across the path by the Church gate and the groom had to pay for him and his bride to pass.

The Church was considerably altered and restored in the 1500s and a further restoration was carried out when the Rev Walter Hook was Rector. The spire was restored in 1884 and the oak shingles replaced. The Church was closed in 1890 and services were held in the schoolroom while another room was specially fitted out and licensed. On May 26th 1891 the Church was reopened by the Lord Bishop of the Diocese. All the money was raised locally and the work was carried out by Messrs Cooksley and Huish. The Parish was justly proud that it was all done by local men. The steeple was again re-shingled in 1933. The shingles are flat pieces of Sussex oak, nine by four inches, used like slates and fixed with copper nails.

Most of the Rectory was built in the early 18th century, but there is evidence that some parts are as early as 14th century. For many years the Rectors held what was known as the Rectory Manor. Part of their living came from the rents of cottages and gardens on this land. It was mainly in Hawkcombe and included the Mill, up as far as Peep Out Cottage, where it turned up to Porlock Hill and then down the road to a point near the Ship Inn, and then back to the Rectory. The New Rectory was built in 1992-3 and the Old Rectory was later sold off.

In the woods in Hawkcombe there are still small walled plots, now overgrown, which were once gardens and smallholdings. Some were used until well after World War Two. Even poultry and pigs were kept there.

In the Rectory garden there are many lovely trees. An interesting one is the mulberry, which is believed to have been planted in 1609 when King James I became alarmed at the money his courtiers were spending on silks imported from France. He encouraged mulberry trees to be widely planted to benefit silk farming in England. A former Rector, the Rev Kirkpatrick, told me that the wrong type of mulberry tree had been planted at Porlock.

The land in Hawkcombe, originally used as allotments by men who sang in the Church choir, is still known as the Alleluia Field. And the hill near the television mast is still known as Parsons Hill.

4

PORLOCK AND THE

MONMOUTH REBELLION

SUPPORT FOR THE DUKE OF MONMOUTH in 1685 came mainly from Dorset, East Devon, South Somerset, and towns such as Chard, Taunton and Frome. Some support came from West Somerset.

The Royalist forces of King James II won the day over this ill-fated, poorly trained army at Weston Zoyland. This last battle on English soil was ever after called the Battle of Sedgemoor. Much has been written of the battle, and its aftermath: the killings by Kirke's Lambs; the dragoons who returned from Tangier and left their name in the Tangier area of Taunton, where they billeted; the trials at Exeter, Dorchester and Taunton, presided over by the notorious Judge Jeffreys. Many men were deported as slaves to the West Indies; others were hung, amongst them five at Minehead, three at Dunster, three at Dulverton and two at Porlock. We don't know where in Porlock, but it can be imagined what the villagers thought and felt. These men had been brought, probably in a cart from Taunton, and hung as a warning to the people in the village never again to risk defying the King. The men were named as James Gale, a weaver of St Mary's, Taunton, accused of aiding the Blue Regiment, and Henry Edney, also of Taunton. Both had been tried at Taunton. They were hanged in December 1685.

In the 1960s, during some alterations at Red Rose Cottage, the home of Mr Frank Norman at the west end of the village (situated opposite Rose Bank, the cottage has since been demolished), a sword was discovered sealed into a recess. It turned out to be an old English broadsword. At the time it was suggested that it was hidden after the Rebellion as it would have been a serious offence to have a weapon of that sort in one's possession.

5

THE LIME KILNS

THERE WERE ONCE many lime kilns in the area, both on farms and along the coast. The most prominent one in the Porlock area is on Bossington Beach. One now built over was at Porlock Weir, where the fireplaces can still be seen. Another is at the bottom of Worthy Water, where it joins the beach. There are others at Lynmouth, Glenthorne, Lee Bay, Woody Bay, Heddons Mouth and Watchet, and there was one at Minehead.

Where land was too acid, lime, which is very alkaline, was added by farmers to improve the soil. At one time a substance known as marl was used; this is a type of rock that consists of almost equal amounts of calcium carbonate and clay. There were marl pits at Middlecombe, near Minehead, and at Blackford Farm, west of Brakeley Steps, near the Porlock road.

It was later that lime was used. There were some outcrops locally at Newlands, near Exford, but as these were few lime was imported to West Somerset and North

The old lime kiln at Bossington Beach.

Devon from South Wales, particularly from Aberthaw, near Barry. It was brought over in sailing ketches in the form of limestone, as it had been quarried. Where the kiln was near a harbour, the boat would come in and offload, but where there was no harbour, as at Bossington, the boat would get as near to the shore as was safe and the cargo would be thrown overboard at high tide. As the tide ebbed a horse and cart, or donkeys with panniers or crucks, were used to bring the stones to the kiln.

The kiln consisted of a strong stone building surrounding a huge pit, about sixteen feet deep and eight feet in diameter. Underneath were two or sometimes three archways. It was from these archways that the lime, when molten, was dropped from a type of flue. The firing took several days. The method was to burn the limestone with the culm (pronounced 'cullum' locally), an anthracite dust, also imported from Wales.

The lime kiln at Porlock Weir, which had a house built on it after the Second World War.

The fire was lit with brushwood at the bottom of the flue to get the culm started, then the alternative layers of broken limestone and culm, which had been fed down the pit, would burn and get red hot. After several days, when the firing was complete and the lime was cool enough, it would be raked out at the bottom of the kiln and taken away, again by donkeys at the more inaccessible places, or by pack ponies or horses and carts at others.

The lime was also used in the building trade for lime mortar, and for lime wash for both interior and exterior walls. Lime mortar was made by adding about three times its volume of sand and mixing it with water.

Lime-spreading was very hard work, and both men and horses often suffered burns. The lime was taken to the fields in horse-drawn butts, dropped in heaps and then spread by hand.

Lime has been used to sweeten the acid soil for over a thousand years; it neutralises the acidity and improves clay soil. Slaked lime was extensively used on Exmoor by the Knights' tenants when they first cleared the land. Exmoor, with its peat bogs, is notoriously acid, and it was found that it required about one ton of lime per acre. A footpath above Porlock Weir leading to the moors is still known as Lime Way.

Lime-burning certainly continued into the 19th century. An old Exford man told me he had hauled lime from Porlock Weir to Exford, then spread it on the fields. At Bossington the exact date lime-burning ceased is unknown, but there was a lime-burner recorded in the 1851 Bossington census. I expect the burning carried on until much later. At Bossington today you can find pieces of lime and small pieces of culm scattered around the old kiln, and the old stone walls there are held together with lime mortar.

In the 1920s and 1930s more use was made of sulphate of amonia, basic slag and superphosphates – all in bags, thus easing the farmer's work and putting the lime-burner out of business.

The list of harbour dues at Porlock Weir dated 5th March 1723 includes: 'for every ton of Lime Stone 0s.1d.'

6

THE TANYARD

Unloading the bark at the Tannery.

TANNING WAS AN INDUSTRY which provided employment for several hundred years in the area. Mention is made of tanners, and also the appointment of inspectors of leather in the Court Leat, as early as the reign of James I.

In later days the Tannery was owned by Mr Pearce, and after him by his son. The town Mill, next to the Castle Inn, was rebuilt in 1898 for the purpose of producing electricity for the Tannery.

To extract the tan from the bark of the indigenous sessel oak trees from the surrounding

Stripping the bark from oak trees for the Tannery, c1920.

The Tannery workforce pose for a photo in 1914. Note the tan pits.

woodlands, men would cut the trees in springtime and, with a special iron tool known as a bark-stripper, remove the bark from the wood. The remaining wood was used for firewood and fencing posts, and the tree stumps were left to re-sprout and grow again for future use. These oak woods were known as scrub oak.

Various men would buy what was known as a 'rap of wood' for this purpose.

After ripping off the bark and drying it, the bark would be taken to the Tannery where, near the entrance, was a weighbridge and office. It was stored in large sheds until wanted, and would then be ground up on a machine driven by a large waterwheel from the Mill Leat.

The hides were first soaked in a lime pit for about two weeks to loosen the hair sufficiently for unhairing, using scrapers. The hair was sold to the building trade for mixing with plaster. Afterwards the hides were thoroughly washed and then the fleshers would remove all the fat and flesh by scraping with two-handled fleshing knives.

The ground-up oak bark was soaked in pits, then the hides were soaked in the liquid and continually moved into fresh solutions for about twelve months. Then they would be hung to drip before being rolled. The tannin (tannic acid) from the oak bark seeps very slowly through the pores of the hide and drives out water, coating the fibres with preservatives.

There was always a burning heap of used bark in a field below the village. It gave off an obnoxious smell, as did the hides.

The pits were situated in what is now the garden of the hardware shop, the house butting on to the street being the house of Mr Pearce, the tanner. Altogether about thirty men were employed. The hours were long, from six in the morning until six at night, a bell summoning the men to work and to finish. There was an early finish at 4pm on Saturdays, and no work on Sundays.

When anyone who lived in the High Street was seriously ill, a thick layer of tan from the Tannery would be spread in the road outside the house; this deadened the sound of the horses and wagon wheels. Apparently people were very considerate about noise disturbance, perhaps more so than nowadays.

Porch House, c1900.

The leather produced, which was of top quality, was used to make harnesses and hunting equipment; and a small quantity of the best leather was used for footwear. The Tannery was closed in the early 1930s.

On one occasion, when the firm had its outing to London, some of the men paid a visit to a pub for refreshment and, in the course of conversation with a barmaid, one asked if she was busy. 'Not particularly,' she replied. 'I think you will be today,' she was told, 'there's thirty of us up from Porlock.'

During the Second World War the Tannery was taken over as a barracks. The 58th Company of Royal Engineers, many of whom had returned from Dunkirk, arrived in 1941 and stayed until they were sent off to India in 1942. Later the American Army used the barracks, and huts for extra accommodation were built in the field behind the Tannery. These were demolished in 1945, immediately after hostilities ceased in Europe.

The buildings were subsequently used by the Exmoor Engineering Company until that business closed. The site is now divided into apartments, houses, a car park and a medical centre.

7

SMUGGLING

FOR HUNDREDS OF YEARS there was smuggling around the coast of Britain, and particularly in the South of England because it was nearer to the coast of France. Places along the whole length of the Bristol Channel have stories concerned with smuggling. It is mentioned in the Magna Carta, and from that time onward the authorities tried to prevent it, as the loss of revenue was very great. There was certainly smuggling in the Porlock area, although as far as is known there were not, as in some places, any serious clashes with the revenue men.

In some areas smuggling was a highly organised crime, conducted by desperate men using armed luggers of thirteen to twenty tons or more, and using bribery and threats of violence. We know of notorious places nearby: Lynmouth, Watermouth and Ilfracombe, and of course Lundy Island. Heddons Mouth was a favourite landing place; there a smuggling lugger sailed too close to the shore and was lost with all hands. At Trentishoe no less than 262 tubs were found under a stable floor. Minehead and Watchet, too, together with Porlock Weir, had their own resident Excise Officers. The Excise men sometimes changed sides and did a bit of smuggling themselves.

An enquiry made by the Court of Exchequer in 1559 regarding customs dues along the Somerset coast, listing seven ports, describes Porlock Bay: 'Where may ride forty or fifty ships, but there is no Quay nor safe Lying.' Of course Porlock Weir harbour would have been too small for a ship of any size or great draught.

In 1723 Mr William Culliford, Surveyor General of HM Customs, paid a visit to Porlock and this is his report: 'I went to visit Porlock which is about four miles from Mynehead where there is a very deep Bay and a good harbour for small vessels, to which place there are several that belong, which trade over sea. The officer Richard Davis is an active young fellow, hath hitherto been paid £5 per ann, by incident; he well deserves £10 per ann. and be stablished, it being a place of trade and where great quantities of herrings are taken and cured, which begets a great concourse of people and small craft, that may be of dangerous consequence to the Customs, unless well guarded.'

We can be certain that smuggling was carried out at Porlock because temporary hiding places abounded in the area. There was one under the floor at Bromham Farm. While relaying the floor during the 19th century, a Mr Huish of Parson Street was taken into the secret, and undertook the work in one day. In return he was treated as a favoured customer, and was well entertained, and on going home fell into the water, and suffered from gout ever after. In Higher Doverhay Farm there was another such place, contrived between an inner and an outer wall. A second wall had been built outside the main wall of the house at the dairy end. The thatched roof had been brought down to cover the space between the two. The new wall, therefore, looked from the outside like the main wall of the house. The hole was hidden by placing a milk pan before it. When discovered at about the turn of the 20th century, the stands for the spirit kegs were still in place. I have spoken to a builder who helped in the

Doverhay Farm.

work so I know it to be authentic. Miss Clara Ridler, who lived at Doverhay Farm, told me that the little window in the chimney by the front door of the farm was used as a look-out to Porlock Weir, a signal being made between Doverhay Farm and the boats in the bay if the coast was clear. Nowadays Porlock Weir cannot be seen from this window as houses have been built opposite which block the view.

Another hiding place was found in about 1850 when a hunted hare disappeared below ground near Pools Wood and Bossington Lane. By digging the hole was made big enough for a man to enter and below he found a chamber nine or ten feet square, and over the height of a man. I was very interested when a friend who lived in Old Lane told me that he knew where this hiding place was. The electricity company wanted to put a stay just inside his garden, to support a post outside. He asked if they were going to dig the hole by hand. They said no, they would use a digger. When they brought the digger and the work started, the ground collapsed and the digger dropped down into a hole which he described as being a little room lined with bricks. Whether this was the same hole as the one previously described I don't know, but it is in the same area. It has now been filled in.

Many other reported hiding places have been found at West Porlock and Porlock Weir. There was a story about an old lady at Chapel Knapp. When the Customs men came searching, she sat on top of a keg, and said, 'Come inside, me dears, you be welcome to search here.' They searched and found nothing, but of course her long skirt was draped over the keg.

It was reported that in 1886 great casks of rum, together with thousands of coconuts, came ashore following the wrecking, off the Nash, of the vessel *Mabel*. The Customs Officers made their grab but they missed a lot, for men of the Weir had already tapped some of the casks and filled smaller kegs from them, hiding them in Culbone Woods. Rebecca Pollard of Porlock Weir hid a cask in her garden and covered it with a skep of bees, knowing that if they came the Customs men wouldn't likely disturb the bees.

I remember when up to a dozen very large barrels of wine were washed ashore, and were picked up and taken to a lock-up at Pollard's Garage. The Customs and Excise men came and put their seal on the barrels. However, sad to say, the sea water had got into what, in any case, was cheap wine, so the whole lot was just drained out into the paddock. I suspect that in those days the barrels would have been taken ashore without the Customs Officers even knowing about them.

8
TWO POETS AND A CENSUS

PICTURE IN YOUR MIND the Porlock of 8th August 1799, when the Poet Laureate Robert Southey stayed at the Ship Inn. During his stay he described Porlock as a place known as the end of the world to some folk because there was no road for wheeled vehicles beyond it. The hill farms were still using sleds to move hay for fodder and bedding for the animals. The weather must have been bad, as the rain kept him inside by the ale-house fire, in a spot still known as 'Southey's Corner'. Whilst he was confined indoors he wrote the Sonnet to Porlock which was published in the *Morning Post* on August 26th 1799.

> Porlock, thy verdant vale so fair to sight,
> Thy lofty hills which fern and furze embrown.
> The waters that roll musically down
> Thy wooded glens, the traveller with delight
> Recalls to memory, and the Channel grey
> Circling its surges in thy level bay.
> Porlock, I also shall forget thee not,
> Here by the unwelcome summer rain confined,
> But often shall hereafter call in mind
> How here, a patient prisoner, 'twas my lot
> To view the lonely, lingering close of day,
> Making my sonnet by the ale-house fire
> Whilst idleness and solitude inspire
> Dull rhymes to pass the duller hours away.

The poet Coleridge, a contemporary of Southey and Wordsworth, lived for a time at Nether Stowey. During this time he walked with his friends on the Quantocks and on Exmoor. It was while he was staying in the summer of 1797 at a lonely farm (believed to be Ash Farm)

between Porlock and Lynmouth, writing his poem 'Kubla Khan', that a visitor, 'a man from Porlock', called, and by so doing broke his train of thought. The lines were lost forever; the poem was never finished. The man from Porlock is reprimanded for all time by lovers of poetry.

Now let us jump forward to the mid-19th century, when the population of Porlock was a little larger, most people working on the land and living in cottages. There were a few shopkeepers. The following is an extract from the 1851 census of that time:

Population of whole Parish = 854
Porlock Town = 448
Bossington = 128

The census of 1851 was the first to ask for everyone's birthplace. Of the 176 heads of families and their wives

in Porlock and Bossington, 47 per cent were born outside Porlock. Only 9 people were over 70, the oldest a man of 82. There were 111 children in Porlock town, of whom 76 were listed as scholars. The age range was between 4 and 13.

OCCUPATION – PORLOCK TOWN

Farming	33
Labourers	27
House Servants	13
Charwomen	2
Artist	1
Masons	15
Carpenters	6
Thatchers	2
Painter	1
Mariners	2
Tanners	2
Bootmakers	4
Cordwainers	9
Relieving Officer	1
Blacksmiths	5
Coopers	4
Rector and Groom	2
Tailors	7
Dressmakers	7
Drapers	3
Seamstress	1
Straw Bonnet-Maker	1
Shop-keepers	3
Innkeepers	5
Millers	2
Bakers	3
Cheese-Dealers	2
Tallow-Chandlers	2
Carrier	1
Teachers	3
Doctor	1
Letter Carriers	1
Sawyers	2
Out of Service	4

The Ship Inn, Porlock, then and now, 1900 and 2009.

9

TALES MY GRANDPARENTS TOLD ME

As a small boy I remember my Grandfather telling me he could remember Porlock Market days. There were three annual Fairs, in May, August and October, and also a weekly Market. He said the sheep and bullocks were penned all along the street, near the Castle Inn. At one time there were as many as fifteen hundred sheep and two hundred bullocks. The hurdles were stored, when not in use, in a building where the Central Garage now is. In the 19th century people spoke of a Market House similar to that at Dunster, and a Market Cross. It is likely that the arrival of the railway at Minehead put a stop to Porlock Market, and certainly with the coming of motor cars a street market would be impossible as Porlock has only the one through road.

Grandfather went to school in Parson Street, where the fee was 3d per day. The schoolmaster was Mr John Orchard, who lived in Doverhay. It should be noted that in those days families stayed in areas for generations. Porlock was no exception. There was a John Orchard recorded as living in Doverhay in the 14th century, in the 21st year of King Henry III. A new school was opened in 1876. This is now the Visitor Centre, Library and the Lovelace Computer Centre. The present school was built in a part of the Old Rectory grounds and opened in 1993.

Visitor Centre at the Old School – bicycle stand by Jim Horrobin.

As a boy Grandfather was employed, as many boys were all over England in Queen Victoria's reign, in bird-scaring. The corn was either sown broadcast by hand, or with a fiddle; corn drills were not used then, at least not on very steep hillsides. After the corn was sown he would stay on Parsons Hill, scaring away crows, rooks and so on for a penny a day. The boys used either a rattle, similar to those still used by football supporters these days, or a clapper, which consisted of two flat pieces of wood joined by a piece of leather – with a quick flick of the wrist the two pieces would slap together and make a loud report like a gun. The boys would shout and wave their arms about too. Grandfather always used a clapper.

Grandmother's uncle, George Jarman, was a carrier for Lynch Flour Mills. Some of his deliveries with his wagon and two horses took him over Porlock Hill to Lynmouth. Once he was attacked by robbers on his way home and he had to use his whip on them. After that occasion, when he was paid for the flour he used to put the money into the corner of a flour bag and put it on the wagon with all the other bags on top of it.

Grandfather used to tell me that the Lord and Lady whose statue is in the Church were killed by a wild boar, which came out of Pools Wood, near Bossington Lane. This story was used sometimes to frighten young children who misbehaved. In all probability the story arose because the Lady has her feet resting on a boar, which was the badge of the Courtenay family.

Grandmother's family lived at Bossington. In the days when smuggling was rife, sometimes the sound of horses and carts would be heard coming up from the beach at night. The curtains would be tightly drawn so that no one saw anything. That way, if they were questioned, a truthful answer could be given: nothing had been seen. The families of both my Grandparents were staunch Wesleyans and services were held in the front room of their home at Bossington before the Chapel was built. John Wesley himself preached strongly against the smuggling trade. It was Rudyard Kipling who wrote, in his smuggling song:

Them that asks no questions, isn't told a lie,
Watch the wall, my darling, while the gentlemen go by.

My Great Grandparents John and Sarah Burgess lived at the lower of the two Ship Cottages, at the bottom of Redway, just above the Ship Inn. One day a man travelling with a performing bear came and asked for lodging for the night, which they agreed to provide. 'What shall I do with the bear?' asked the man. 'Put him in the empty sty,' he was told. There were two sties at the top of the garden, one for each cottage, but at the time there was only one in use. During the night the bear broke through the wall, and killed and ate the pig which was in the other sty.

My Grandfather often related the story of the Lynmouth Lifeboat, of which so much has been written. The men of Lynmouth brought the lifeboat *Louisa* over the hills and down to Porlock Weir and launched it from there one winter night in 1899 when the full-rigged, nineteen-hundred-ton *Forest Hall* of Liverpool was in distress in Porlock Bay. He was out early making his bread deliveries when the boat arrived. Just before this, when the boat on its carriage reached the two cottages on what is still, I expect, the narrowest part of the A39 (it was even narrower in those days), it was found that they couldn't get through, so the men began to knock off the corner of the top cottage wall. The story goes that the old lady living in the cottage looked out of the window and shouted, 'What be you about down there?' She was told of the ship in distress, and assured that they would take only a little bit off her

Dovery Manor Museum, restored 2009.

wall and would come back later to repair it. She decided to get up; she had never seen a lifeboat before, so followed it to Porlock Weir. The story of the epic launch was related for years by the older folk of Porlock; it was probably the greatest event in their lives. The story has been described in books and on TV, and there are displays at the National Park Information Centre at Lynmouth and at Dovery Manor Museum in Porlock.

It was after this event that a lifeboat station was built at Minehead in 1901, thus lessening the distance between stations. Grandfather often spoke of another event, the great snow of 1891, when Amos Cann lost his life. The Canns lived at Greenlands Farm, near Exford, and Amos had walked to Porlock on business. It was snowing hard in the evening when he left to walk home. Local people begged him to stay the night, but he insisted on returning as he was needed to tend the sheep. He didn't arrive home. Searchparties and the staghounds were used to try to find him, but it was seventeen days later that his body was discovered under a hedge, near Alderman's Barrow, about a mile from his home. It was thought that he had fallen into a snow-drift and been too exhausted to get out. There is a headstone to his grave just inside the Churchyard at Exford. I met his brother Sam, who came to live in Por-lock when he was an old man. He was nearly ninety when I spoke to him.

People often had to travel long distances to work, but had no transport. Two of my Grandfather's brothers were builders at Porlock. At one time they were building some houses at Barbrook Mill, above Lynmouth. They would work each week from Monday to Saturday midday, staying in lodgings. On Saturday afternoon they walked the fourteen or fifteen miles to their homes, spent the evening and all of Sunday with their wives, and early on Monday walked to Barbrook to work again. The Pollard brothers of Porlock Weir

also walked to and from Lynmouth for boat-building work. One man walked daily from Selworthy to Exford and back, and more recently I well remember an old man walking from Selworthy to Porlock for gardening work when he was well over seventy years old. Life was tough in those days.

Life was also hard for young people. Grandfather's oldest brother, William, started work at the age of eleven at Wydon Farm, near Minehead. Grandfather could remember seeing how a local chimney-sweep would climb up inside to sweep the larger chimneys. When he reached the top, he would look out and shout, 'Sweep all up!'

Grandfather was one of the village bakers and used to bake and deliver bread around the village. He told me that in his early days he had to go to Bristol for the first time, to learn the trade, and he asked: 'How shall I know the way?' The answer was: 'You've got a civil tongue in your head, haven't you?'

He bought his flour at Lynch Flour Mills, which closed in about 1890. The bread was risen with the aid of barm from the Sparkhayes Malt House. A portion of dough was kept each day, in order to be put into the new ferment to help it to rise. It was made in the evening and left until about 3 am, when work would start.

During the First World War they said they ate black bread – not really black, but very dark. In order to save flour, they added a proportion of boiled potatoes to the mixture.

Grandfather told me of the big snowfall of his young days, when, with the bread in a basket, he had to walk to Bossington along the tops of the hedges as the lane was full of snow. There were no houses in Bossington Lane so there was no one to clear the snow. Another baker who had a bakehouse in Parson Street was Mr Brewer. He used to deliver bread to Porlock Weir, walking all the way with a basket on each arm.

10

METHODISM IN PORLOCK

GEORGE WHITFIELD was the first Methodist preacher to visit Somerset when, in 1739, he preached at Keynsham and Publow. John Wesley preached at Bath on 10th April 1739.

Wesley's prime concern was to bring his message to the working people. It is for this reason that Methodism was at its strongest in Somerset in the mining villages and cloth-making towns of the county, mostly in the Mendips.

At first Wesley's preaching was opposed by the mob, who were often encouraged by Anglican clergymen. However, undaunted, he continued, and visited the county every Autumn until 1790, the year before his death. Sometimes the preaching of Wesley and his followers fell on deaf ears. At Wincanton he thought the people had as much feeling as the benches they sat on.

Wesley and his preachers persevered, and it is estimated that he preached 540 sermons in at least forty towns and villages in Somerset in fifty-one years. The only place in Somerset west of Bridgwater that he visited was Minehead, on two occasions.

By 1790 the Methodists were established in Taunton. Mr Giles, a tanner from Holnicote, persuaded the Taunton preacher to include this part of West Somerset in his pastorate and regular meetings were held at Williton, Carhampton and Holnicote. In Porlock the earliest preachers came and preached in the main street and in Sparkhayes Lane, standing either on a mounting block or on a chair.

By 1811 the new Dunster Circuit had been established. This included Porlock, where services were held

The Old Chapel with a floral arch erected to celebrate 100 years of the Sunday School, 1826-1926.

in local homes. In 1826 there was a membership of six, plus adherents, who met in a room of Mr Nicholas Snow's cottage, opposite the present Church. The Porlock Methodist Society grew until, in 1836, with a membership of thirty, it was decided to build a Chapel. There was already a strong Sunday School which had started in 1826, and by 1851 had 65 members. There was also a day school.

A site was leased from the Earl of Lovelace at £1 per annum for a term of sixty years. A Chapel to seat 170 was completed in 1837 at a cost of £225. The freehold was obtained in 1885 when the Earl sold Sparkhayes and other properties. The building is now the Olde Chapel restaurant and tea room.

A postcard showing the Old Chapel, c1900-10.

The first steward was George Rawle, master tanner, the son-in-law of Nicholas Snow. Memorials to George Rawle and his wife Mary are on the wall at the back of the present Church.

By 1908 the Porlock Methodists, or, as they were by then more commonly called, Wesleyans, decided to build a new Church and acquired a piece of land opposite the Post Office. But fund-raising was slow, and there was a constant migration of Methodist families to Minehead and further away. Once World War One came there was no possibility of building until, in the 1920s, a new spirit came to the members and they began to raise money by subscription and many fund-raising efforts. The last service in the Old Chapel was in March 1927; then for three months services were held in the Village Hall. The new Church was designed by Mr Tamlyn, a Minehead architect, and built by Brown Brothers of Porlock, a Methodist family, at a cost of £4,600.

The Church is built of red sandstone from West Luccombe Quarry, a gift of the Acland family of Holnicote, and the building is faced with Bath stone. It was opened in June 1927 and the opening sermon was preached by the Rev Dr Ferrier Hulme, then President of the Methodist Conference. Afterwards tea was served in the Village Hall to nearly five hundred people in three relays.

After tea there was an evening meeting presided over by Mr William Stoate of Williton, another great name in Methodism. The Church, with seating for 350, was packed and chairs had to be put in the aisles. Over four hundred attended and over £970 was raised in this one evening.

Laying the foundation stone of the New Chapel, 1926.

The opening of the New Chapel, June 1927.

There are extensive rooms below the Church, and a schoolroom at the rear of the building. The premises have been well used over the years, both by the Church and by various other village organisations.

In 1939 a new Hammond electronic organ was purchased to replace the old hand-pumped instrument. In 1970 the Hammond was replaced by a pipe organ from Sunnyside Methodist Church, Weston-super-Mare, which had become redundant. The organ, built in 1888 by Walker of London, was rebuilt at Porlock by Messrs George Osmond, Organ Builders of Taunton. The Church was filled for the opening recital given by Dudley Savage, the popular radio organist. This organ had the traditional tracker action with the addition of a balanced swell pedal; it had two manuals and a full pedal board. In 2007 it was removed and replaced by a modern electronic organ.

In 1981 the area for worship in the Church was altered by the removal of several rows of pews. The wood from these was used to make a movable screen. The back area is now a useful lounge. Later, in a major refurbishment, the rest of the pews were replaced by chairs to make the worship area more flexible.

Many people have served the Church well, and many of the Sunday School scholars have gone out into the wider world to help to spread the gospel in their work. Some have gone as preachers, some even as missionaries and doctors to places as far afield as India.

Many local preachers were men and women from Porlock. They would often travel by horse or pony trap in all weathers to take services in small chapels in the Circuit, usually taking two or even three services on a Sunday – this after working all week. Later on local preachers and ministers often travelled by bicycle, bus or car, depending on the generosity of local people for meals during their visits. Circuit meetings were also far away, and had to be attended. It is often not realised that in the Methodist Church each Sunday only one in seven preaching appointments is taken by a trained minister, although local preachers also have to study

The new Chapel soon after completion.
The notice board announces services at the Village Hall.
Note the mounting block outside, used by the postmaster.

for exams before becoming fully accredited preachers.

Porlock Methodist Church is one of the sixteen churches which, since 1969, form the West Somerset Circuit, an amalgamation of the former Kingsbrompton, Minehead, Dunster and Williton Circuits. The number of churches has now been reduced to ten.

It is the desire of the Porlock Methodists that their Church building should be used by Christian folk and others for many years to come.

11

A SALE, A FIRE AND A COURT CASE

ON SATURDAY 17th September 1887 at two o'clock at the Ship Inn there was held a large auction sale of building sites and property in Porlock and Luccombe (Luccombe meaning Dovery). This property was owned by Mr Blathwayt, the owner of Porlock Manor Estate. As the properties were of very low rent, I believe it was a way to raise money for the improvements then needed for Porlock Weir harbour, and for building the lock gates. The sale particulars described Lot 1 as two cottages, with garden, piggery etc, situated on the Porlock and Lynton road above the Ship Inn, as now occupied by John Burgess and John Moore at the rent of £3 10s each per annum. John and Sarah Burgess were my Great Grandparents.

Lot 14, in the Parish of Luccombe, was described as the 'Valuable premises known as Lurborn Court', comprising two four-roomed cottages, barn, two-stall stable, three-stall stable and cattle shed with yards, good garden and orchard, held, with other premises, by Mr R. Ridler, at the apportioned rent of £10. On the Porlock side of this property runs the public water course known as Lurborn or the Lowerbourne Water. The owner has the right to use the water for drinking purposes and it is regarded as a public offence to pollute or divert it. This stream is the old boundary stream already described as the division between Dovery and Porlock.

In 1900 a disastrous fire destroyed much of this part of Dovery. It started on Shrove Tuesday in the house occupied by Mr Robert Powell, opposite the Wesley Chapel. Apparently a beam in the chimney caught fire (many cottage fires have started this way) and the fire quickly spread to the cattle shed and stables behind the cottage. There was no Porlock fire brigade, so all the able-bodied men formed a bucket chain down the main street from the mill stream. Eventually a fire engine arrived, probably the one kept by the Acland family at Holnicote. A hand-pumped machine, it needed three men each side pushing a bar up and down. The house and several other buildings were destroyed.

Luckily the two houses at the top of Sparkhayes Lane abutting on the Wesley Chapel had just been built, so Mr Ridler of Sparkhayes Farm offered the top house to Mr Powell to rent as the first tenant.

Lowerbourne was eventually rebuilt by the new owner, Mr Philip Arnold. He also built the grocer's and draper's shop known as Lowerbourne House. Two new rows of cottages were built in Lowerbourne.

Today Porlock appears as a clean and tidy village, but it is only since 1960 that the cow sheds have been gone from Sparkhayes Lane. Before that cows were regularly driven up the lane from the fields for milking. Cows were also driven up the Porlock Weir road from the marsh to Court Place Farm.

In a court case in 1903 concerning pollution of a property in Porlock, the Judge, in his summing up, described the village thus: 'It has been said that life is a series of disappointments and disillusions, and certainly I have been disillusioned regarding Porlock. I have always thought it was a rural village with no smells about it, but the ozone from the ocean. But now, from what I have heard, it appears to be a very filthy

village, one of the filthiest in Somersetshire.' Down to 1889 there had been no vestige of drainage of any kind whatever, and now it appeared there was drainage only for fifteen cottages. The rest of the village remained in the condition in which it had been from the earliest days: all the filth was thrown into the open stream. 'Fortunately it is not a town. In small villages people can endure a great deal of detrimental smell without danger to their health. But', the Judge thought, 'few strangers who know of this state of things will now be induced to go there in search of ocean breezes.'

Fire at Lowerbourne, 1900, tackled with a bucket chain and hand pump only.

37

Flood in the High Street, 1960.
Many shops and houses were flooded out.

The Judge's description of Porlock shows how it was at that time. The main stream is now quite clean, although it was very polluted and full of rubbish not so many years ago, despite notices to the effect that anyone throwing rubbish in the river would be fined £5.

In 1960 there was severe flooding in Porlock, and many shops and houses in the main street suffered. Afterwards a great deal of money was spent on flood protection measures, which included the widening of the Hawkcombe Stream and deepening of the culvert under the main street. Now the stream is kept quite clean.

The Judge's comment that, because the people lived in a small village they could endure bad smells without detriment to health, does not ring true because prior to that time many children had died of diseases such as diphtheria when there had been epidemics in Porlock. It was because of this that Porlock's first piped water supply came in 1876. Thirteen standpipes were placed at strategic points throughout the village: outside Dovery Court, at the bottom of Lowerbourne and opposite the Ship Inn. One of the causes of pollution was a pack of hounds kept by Mr Henry Phelps at the back of Bridge House. The kennels drained into the stream, which was commonly called the Raggle.

These hounds were reputedly foxhounds. I have been told, though, that they were very unruly and would chase cats and squirrels alike. One day when they were passing through the village street and an old lady had the top half of her hatch door open, a hound jumped in and took a pound of butter. The lady shouted to the huntsman, 'Mr Phelps, that hound has stolen a pound of butter!' Quick as a flash Mr Phelps replied, 'Don't worry, missus, a bit of butter won't hurt him.'

The hounds were eventually sold to Mr Nicholas Snow of Oare, who was Master of the Hunt for twenty years. The pack, known as The Stars of the West, were the forerunners of the Exmoor Foxhounds.

The Central Garage office fire, 1937. Help was by bucket chain until Minehead Fire Brigade arrived. It was after this event that Porlock formed a Fire Brigade with a pump towed by a lorry from the garage.

12

THE GOLF COURSE

On a Friday afternoon in August 1910 the new Golf Links on Porlock Marsh were formally opened by the Countess of Lovelace, who was the President of the Club. The links were provided by an enterprising company of enthusiasts calling themselves the Porlock Golf Company and many people had taken an interest by taking up shares at 5s each. The nine-hole course was laid out by Messrs Huish and Cooksley, builders, on Mr Blathwayt's land, under the direction of Mr Benge, a golf professional. Bunkers and access bridges, some still there, were built, with the only access down Sparkhayes Lane. At the bottom there was a raised path through the fields, should the lane be too muddy. It was hoped to improve the lane later so that the inevitable motor car could go right to the bottom, thus avoiding a long walk for the members before they started to play.

Sir Francis Gould remarked, proposing a vote of thanks to Lady Lovelace, that the course was in the 'most charming place … It does

Remains of the Golf House on Porlock Marsh, c1970.

not take very long, even to a casual visitor to Porlock, to get attached to this beautiful place.' Two foursome parties played the first game, and afterwards tea was provided by Mrs S. Stenner of Porlock. There was a club house (now a ruin) where the players could leave their clubs under the care of the professional Mr Benge, and another club house in the village, opposite the Castle Hotel, which was used for social activities.

It was planned to increase the course to eighteen holes later, but unfortunately that autumn the high tides brought the sea in, which washed away most of the Golf Course, dashing any further hopes of using it as a tourist attraction.

Had the Golf Course been a success, had the marsh not been prone to occasional flooding, is it possible that Porlock would have developed towards the sea, with vehicular access to a sea front with shops and entertainments, as has happened along so much of our English coastline.

13

PORLOCK MURDER CASE

STRANGE SHOOTING FATALITY IN A SOMERSETSH RE VILLAGE

OLDER PEOPLE have often spoken of a murder which occurred in the village on Wednesday 3rd June 1914, just before 6 o'clock. It was when Harry Quartley shot Henry (Tacker) Pugsley. The illustrated *Police News* of 11th June 1914 has a centre-page artist's impression of the event and reports as follows:

VILLAGE TRAGEDY.
STARTLING SHOOTING CASE
AT PORLOCK.

The quiet West Somerset Village of Porlock has been dramatically disturbed by a shooting tragedy from behind a garden hedge, ending in the death of a resident, Henry Pugsley, and in the attempted suicide of the alleged assailant, Henry Quartley, another villager, who is said to have borne a grudge against the victim. Some stray pellets from the gun with which the tragedy was committed struck a young woman named Alice Middleton, but her injuries did not prove to be of a serious character. Pugsley's assailant subsequently attempted to shoot himself but a local constable prevented him from doing so and took him to the Police Station.

Quartley is alleged to have said to a Superintendant Perry when he was arrested, 'I shot him, that is straight, that is the truth, so there is an end of it.' 'How long did he live? Are you sure he is dead? Where did it touch him? Have you seen him?'

A curious note, it is said, was found scribbled on a scrap of paper in Quartley's pocket to this effect: 'I got no grievance against no one else, only those two Pugsleys. They were the most dangerous crew I ever knew, and have only got to thank themselves, as they started it.'

He is fifty-five years of age, unmarried, and by trade a mason, but he is possessed of private means left by his father. He owns a house property, living with an unmarried sister in one of his own cottages, and he used the gun for sporting purposes.

Pugsley's house on the right, with a sign over the shop, c1938.

Several people have told me their memories of the event. The Pugsleys lived in a cottage, one of two now demolished to make the car park opposite the Victoria Rooms in Parson Street. Sid Rawle remembered the incident very well: he was coming out of the door of the billiard room opposite the Pugsleys' house when the shot was fired. Clifford Burgess was outside his father's baker's shop cleaning his new bicycle when the shot went off. Of course, the village policeman was soon on the scene, as were quite a number of spectators. Pugsley had staggered indoors, and there died.

Henry Quartley had fired over the garden wall just up the road. He then went to his own house on the opposite side and went upstairs.

Constable Greedy's attention was diverted from the scene by the sound of a shot coming from Quartley's house. Greedy hurried in and went quickly upstairs. He found Quartley's sister, Emily, in a bedroom. She was startled to see him, but warned him with, 'Look out, Mr Greedy, else he will shoot you too.'

Quartley stood in a curtained recess holding his gun. Mr Greedy jumped at him, knocking the gun from his hands, got him on his back on the floor and shouted for help. Two men came up the stairs and the handcuffs were quickly on Quartley's wrists. Quartley had come close to killing himself, but had just missed his face; the shot had left a hole in the ceiling. The prisoner

41

was quickly conveyed to Dunster Po1ice Station, the local headquarters, and from there to Exeter Prison. An inquest was held later at the Victoria Rooms and a trial at the Somerset Assize at Wells on 20th October 1914.

It was a very short trial. Quartley insisted on his guilt and all efforts to persuade him to accept counsel failed. The Judge had no alternative but to pronounce sentence of death. Henry Quartley was hanged at 8 am on Tuesday 10th November. PC Joseph Greedy's bravery in tackling an armed man was recognised by the award of the King's Police Medal.

It seems that this terrible tragedy was the culmination of a much smaller quarrel during the previous year, which resulted in the Pugsleys taking Quartley to court for using indecent language in their house and within hearing of the public highway. The case was dismissed because of lack of evidence.

Quartley, who like his victim had been well respected in the village, brooded over the quarrel and things went from bad to worse until something snapped in Quartley and a terrible vengeance was taken.

14

PORLOCK HILL

EXCEPT FOR THE FACT that everyone driving up or down Porlock Hill today realises that it is very steep, most people, with their powerful cars and good brakes, take little notice of it. But it is world famed. Many older people will remember, as I do, that whenever you were away, maybe in the forces, you only had to mention that you were from Porlock and almost everyone said they had heard of Porlock Hill. 'As steep as Porlock Hill?' was the West Country query when any steep piece of road was mentioned.

No one knows when this route out of Porlock was first used. Some local historians have suggested that Burley Lane from Parson Street was the old packhorse way out towards Lynmouth and the hill farms. The historian Collinson, writing in 1791, says of the Porlock area: 'Most of the roads are so poor and the fields so steep that no carriages of any kind can be used. All the crops are therefore carried in crooks on horses and the manure in wooden pots called dossels.' Robert

The one-in-four section of Porlock Hill, c1970.

Southey wrote of Porlock in 1797: 'This place is called in the neighbourhood "The End of the World". All beyond is inaccessible to carriage, or even cart. A sort of sledge is used by the country people, resting upon two poles like cart shafts.'

In 1812 the condition of the road over Porlock Hill was such that the inhabitants of Porlock were presented at Quarter Sessions for failing to keep it in repair. The present way approaching the hill has always been known as Redway, which could have meant just 'roadway', or it may have been because of the colour of the road when heavy rain brought the red soil down. At one time the people living in the cottages killed and dressed their pigs at

43

A stagecoach ready to climb Porlock Hill, c1900.

shepherd from Court Place Farm riding up to tend his sheep at Holmbush. He always cantered up the one-in-four part between the first and second bend, perhaps finding it easier than walking.

We must not forget the coaching days. The first stagecoach went up the hill in 1843, as witnessed by Mr W. Symons, who in his book *Early Methodism in West Somerset* writes, 'It was my lot to charter the first stagecoach to appear in Porlock, the occasion being a special excursion to the side of the road. All the blood and waste would go down the stream, which was then an open gutter at the roadside. There wasn't so much worry about hygiene then.

The hill wasn't tarred at the steepest part until 1930, and then no steamroller could roll it in; it was done by hand, and then later still with a hand-roller. On a hunting day all the horses and spare horses with their grooms would be ridden up Porlock Hill; there were no horse-boxes. Hunting was nearly as hard for the horses as it was for the deer. Sometimes over a hundred riders would be out. Cart-horses also used the hill. I well remember a

Stagecoach rounding the second bend on Porlock Hill, 1898.

44

Lynton. While baiting at the Ship, scores of inhabitants surrounded the coach and eagerly read the words painted on the exterior.' The four-in-hand coach never ceased to be one of the sights of Porlock and long before it stopped in the 1920s the boys in the school playground used to crane their necks to see the coach turn the corner up to the Ship Inn, the coachman's horn having warned them of its coming.

I have often spoken to men, including my uncle, who as boys rode a leading horse up the hill. When the coach arrived at the Ship Inn, Mr Rook, the landlord, would hire two horses as leaders from Mr David Ridler of Doverhay Farm, or Mr Isaac Burgess at the Bakery. When the coach was ready to leave, a boy would ride on one of the leaders; the coachman would whip up the leading horses, never his own, and away they would go. Just before the first bend, the coach would stop and the coachman would ask all the able-bodied men to get out and walk. Then he would ask all the ladies under forty to get out. This, of course, would nearly empty the coach, ladies being fussy about revealing their age. The coach would then go up to just above the second bend and

Stagecoach, August 1914.

wait for the passengers. When all were aboard again they would proceed to the level just above Whitstones, where they would unhitch the leaders and thank the boy, who usually got a tip at this point. The coach would then drive on while the boy took the leaders back to Porlock. On reaching Culbone Stables – or, as it was then known, Yearnor Moor – the horses would be changed for the journey onward.

Many interesting tales have been told of the exploits of the boys who rode the leaders. My uncle, Clifford Burgess, told me that he used to leave a piece of old hoop iron under the heather at Whitstones so that he could scrape off the lather from the horses before returning to Porlock.

Maurice Hobbs, a nephew of Mr Rook at the Ship, while staying there was asked if he would like to ride a leader. Of course he was eager to do so. His uncle said, 'Now, whatever you do at Whitstones, don't get off the horse.' When they got to the top and unhitched the leaders the coachman made a great fuss and told the passengers how good the boy had been to bring them up safely over such a dangerous journey. The passengers, taking it all in and feeling grateful to be safe, started to throw money out for the boy. Some of the money fell to the ground and Maurice, not wanting to miss any, jumped down to pick it up. The horses dashed off and made their way back to Porlock and Maurice had to walk all the way back.

Another story is told of a lad named Charlie who was the butt of practical jokers. Once when he rode a leader up the other lads put shoemakers' wax on the saddle. On arriving at Whitstones Charlie was stuck fast in the saddle. The story goes that they had to cut his breeches to get him off.

Coming down the hill the method of braking was to use a drag or drug shoe, which was a heavy iron fitted under the coach and attached by a chain. It was pushed under one of the back wheels. This locked the wheel and the coach virtually slid down the hill, leaving a deep groove in the road.

In one of the great events in Porlock mentioned earlier, the Lynmouth Lifeboat was brought over the hill in 1899. Instead of using the twenty horses to tow the carriage, they had to use them to hold it back at the steepest part.

In the early days of motoring the road was rough and in heavy rain just red mud. If you even touched your brakes you were liable to slide. The Council workers used to rake the road by hand each week. At the side of the road was a deep ditch and if you were not careful in passing another vehicle you could end up in it, then have to be pulled out.

The first motor car to climb Porlock Hill was driven by G.B. Edge, for a wager, in 1901. The first motorcycle was in 1909. Here is a report from that time:

An articulator lorry overturns and sheds its load of coal, c1970.

A Motor Cycle Mounts Porlock Hill. On the 23rd ult., this widely known hill, which is the steepest main-road hill in England, was successfully scaled by a motor-bicycle, Mr W. Stone of Taunton having the honour of being the first motor cyclist to accomplish this feat. The hill has a gradient of about one in four for a considerable portion and several very difficult corners and rises about 1,200 feet in three miles of its length. The surface is always rough owing to the coach traffic. Mr Stone was mounted on a Charter-Lea frame with 7hp. Peugeot Twin Engine and geared 4½ to one. The time occupied on the ascent was but 6½ minutes and the speed attained on such a gradient can only be described as marvellous, especially as to the manner the engine picked up after each corner, the machine being pedal less. The ascent was witnessed by Messrs King, Duddridge, and Bennett of Taunton and several local people.

In 1928 the first steamroller climbed up, also for a bet. In 1932 the Singer Car Company brought out a little car which was tested on Porlock Hill and was driven up and down a hundred times, non-stop. The company named it the Porlock model. The Daimler Car Company brought their new cars down for testing, loading them more and more until they broke down. After the Second World War Vauxhall and Bedford lorries were also tested in this way, loaded with concrete blocks.

In spite of the gradient, there are few fatal accidents on the hill. In 1950 Alfred Slade, who built the house on the first bend in 1930, went out to pick some flowers from his wall, and a runaway car ran into him and killed him. On another occasion a lady passenger died from a heart attack after descending Porlock Hill.

There have, however, been many other accidents in which people were injured. An armoured car ran away during the war and hit the bank at the top of Conegar Orchard. A car ran away and finished up in Mr Frank Norman's front room at Rose Cottage, and a crippled lady had to be lifted out through the car roof.

Once in 1930 a Western National service bus from Lynmouth, driven by Arthur Priddle, stopped in the village and Mr Priddle went into the Post Office, leaving his bus with the engine running. When the brake pads contracted, after cooling off, the bus continued through the street with no driver. It went on over the bridge until it crashed into a shop. The first that Arthur Priddle knew of this was when a boy ran into the Post Office and called to him, 'Yer, thy bus 'ave run into Burgess's shop window!' Arthur ran down the street to find the front of his bus in the shop and the engine still running.

In the late 1950s a holiday coach ran away and went right

The first bend on Porlock Hill, c1920. Cars often needed help from eager 'pushers'.

through the village, the driver sounding the horn to warn other road users. The coach finally stopped near the War Memorial at Dunster Steep. It was fortunate that the road had been clear. At precisely the same time on the

47

London to Land's End trial, Easter 1923.

following day I spent several minutes sitting in the High Street in a traffic jam. Several years ago a coach driver told me that he was taking a coach full of people up the hill and they were worried as to whether the coach would make it to the top. The driver asked them all to lean forward and this is what they did. On another occasion a coach ran away and finished up in a garden; in the coach sat forty off-duty policemen.

For many years the AA and RAC had patrolmen with motorbikes and sidecars on Porlock Hill every day. They were kept busy with drivers needing assistance, as also were the local garages, who got the bulk of their business in the early days from Porlock Hill breakdowns. The RAC box was originally at the second bend; then it was moved to Holmbush, and finally taken away. The AA box was, and still is, at Pitt Combe Head and is a listed building, the only box of its kind in Somerset. One of the main jobs for the patrolmen was to keep the water butts filled, as so many cars boiled over and would have to stop and be refilled with water when they had cooled down.

In the early days of motoring, when many cars were gravity fed with petrol, the steepness of the hill meant that petrol couldn't reach the carburettor: the answer was to drive up in reverse. Some early cars had a hand throttle on the steering column and drivers would often run along beside their cars, having set the throttle, and steer it from the outside, thus easing the weight in the car. Another problem was lorries with large loads such as hay, which could cause the front wheels to lift off the ground. In later days the biggest problem has been with larger lorries and articulators shedding their loads on the road, or caravans being too heavy for the car to pull. The driver tries to reverse and if he is lucky the caravan only gets stuck in the hedge; if he is unlucky it turns over.

Many people are still terrified of Porlock Hill and won't go up or down. In the early days some drivers were so frightened that local young men would offer to drive their cars up. If a car couldn't make it, a gang of lads would push to get it going. Once started, one or two would jump on to the running board of the car and ride to the top, where they would usually get a tip for their help.

The greatest excitement was at Easter time when the London to Land's End motor trials were on. A tea-room on the first bend was built in 1925 and Mrs Slade and her helpers stayed open all night on Good Friday as the spectators arrived. As many as two thousand would line the hill early on Saturday morning to watch the fun. Vehicles had to stop at the foot of the hill and then restart. Before the road was tarred in 1929-30, stones would fly out from under the driving wheels. After 1931 the motorcycles and sidecars and three-wheelers all had to do Doverhay Hill as a timed circuit, Porlock Hill being by then too easy for them. After going up Doverhay to Woodcocks Ley (the track is now overgrown), they would return via West Luccombe, then go on again to Porlock and up Porlock Hill.

Many people have cycled up Porlock Hill. With others, I have pushed my bike and camping equipment up it when the Porlock Scouts camped at Weirwater. I have also hiked, with another Scout, over the hill to camp at Malmsmead. It was August and a thunderstorm broke out when we were at the foot of the hill, but we continued through thunder and lightning and torrents of rain until we arrived at Oare Church, not having seen another person. It was war time, so nearly all the cars were off the road. That seems incredible when we see the amount of traffic up and down the hill today.

In the 1950s the Milk Marketing Board ran their Round-Britain Race for professional cyclists. One stage of the race was from Weston-super-Mare to Ilfracombe. I stood amongst other spectators on the bank at the second bend and we saw the cyclists come down Dunster Steep in a bunch, go around the corner by the Royal Oak, and then pass the Ship Inn. They soon appeared, all cycling up the hill except one, who ran all the way up with his bike on his shoulder. In the evening I bought a paper to read the results. The first two had arrived at Ilfracombe with only a wheel distance between them, after a ride of about eighty miles.

Snow and ice are a great problem on Porlock Hill. At one time people didn't use their cars so much in winter, and local people seldom ventured over Porlock Hill for fear of getting caught in snow. Now, with efficient car heaters, they use them much more. Drifts can be up to fifteen feet deep on the top of the hill and it is usual to put grit and salt down at the first sign of snow. There have been years when deep snow has meant snow ploughs trying to clear it as far as County Gate, where they hope to meet the Devon clearing team. The only trouble is that the snow will often come

The Doverhay Garage Co and Central Garage in Porlock c1920/30.

again the next night, and high winds will blow it off the moor and back into the road. In the 1920s and 1930s shovels were used by gangs of workmen, but after the war snow ploughs and bulldozers were used. The snow was cut through – I have seen it cut like cheese at Oare Post, about twelve feet in depth, with a wall of snow ahead.

No traffic would be able to go through. In the severe winter of 1963 the road was closed for eight weeks and cars were completely buried near the AA box. Traffic

George Hall, the AA patrolman, at the AA box at Pittcombe Head, 1947.

Clearing snow the hard way, before snow ploughs, 1940.

to Barnstaple had to take the southern route via South Molton. The cost to the Highway Authority was enormous, as it was also to the telephone company. Until the wires were put underground on Porlock Hill, they often blew down in high gales, and just at the time when people were most isolated.

In snowstorms traders have done their utmost to keep the hill farmers' families and villagers of Oare and Brendon supplied with meat, bread and groceries, sometimes riding ponies out when it was impossible to take a van. One local doctor used skis to go to a patient at Oare. When an old

Clearing snow with a bulldozer (the easier way), 1963.

lady died at Oareford and her body had to be brought to Porlock for burial the hill was impassable, but two men were sent with a lorry up the Toll Road. They struggled up as far as Westcott Brake but could go no further, so they waited for

Porlock Hill, 1963.

Centenary climb, 2001. Ben Hammett's 1933 Austin saloon overtakes the 1928 Singer.

ages until they saw the heads of two horses coming towards them through the deep snow. It was a farmer with a horse-drawn cart with the coffin, which was then taken back to Porlock.

In recent years RAF rescue helicopters have been used in emergencies and so many problems have been easily solved. The people of Exmoor now have less fear of isolation and Porlock Hill is no longer the terror that it once was – but it still must be treated with respect.

Often in summer time in the village the smell of burning rubber is quite sickening. This is, of course, brake rubber, for cars stop when there is a traffic hold-up, with smoke pouring from their brakes. The wise driver knows that bottom gear is best for Porlock Hill. Many ignore the warning signs, forgetting that they have not only the family on board, but all their luggage as well – a tremendous weight in a car for such a hill.

In the 1950s or '60s an escape road was made at the second bend. Out-of-control cars can be driven into it, where deep sand will stop them immediately. But it is amazing how many people park their vehicles, stand and watch the traffic and even picnic there on the sand.

15

THE TOLL ROAD AND PARKS

PARKS WERE CREATED by great landowners, for the purpose of hunting deer and other game on their own lands, only under a licence from the King, the forest being the King's hunting preserve. The Porlock Parks were set out in the 1300s during Sir Nigel Loring's Lordship. Bounded by a wall and ditch surmounted by a fence, they have been part of the Porlock Estate ever since. The wall and ditch are still to be seen at the top of the woods. The present owner is Mr Blathwayt.

George Wynter bought Dyrham in Gloucestershire in 1571. He married Anne Brayne of Bristol, daughter of Robert. Their eldest son John married Mary Brouncker of Erlestoke, Wiltshire. He sailed with Sir Francis Drake. His son, Sir George Wynter, succeeded him in 1619 and married Mary, daughter of Edward Rogers of Cannington, Somerset, whose dowry was the Porlock Manor Estate. When Sir George Wynter died in 1638, his son John was only sixteen. When John Wynter grew up he married the daughter of Thomas Gerard of Trent, whose name was Frances. The daughter of John and Frances was Mary, their only child, who on 23rd December 1686 married William Blathwayt, Secretary of State to William III. It was he who built the house of Dyrham, and succeeded into the ownership of Dyrham and Porlock. The Blathwayt family have been owners of the Porlock Estate since 1686. In 1956 Dyrham, the house, furniture and gardens, were acquired by the nation and later transferred to the National Trust. The house and grounds were opened to the public in 1961 and its parkland is protected from development.

The family visited Porlock frequently but did not live here. The first resident was a widow of the fourth Mr Blathwayt, who then married Admiral Douglas. From 1824 they lived in what is now the Cottage Hotel at Porlock Weir. The family house was later moved to West Porlock, where a new house, West Porlock House, was built in about 1920, the stone being quarried behind the house. It is now an hotel.

The old Manor House of Porlock is, without doubt, now represented by the more recent building of Court Place Farm. The old house was destroyed by fire some time in the early 1800s. The Manor Court was held at Court Place. When the Lord of the Manor ceased to reside there, it became the residence of the farmer of the demesne lands. The site chosen for the Lord's house was ideal, being in a central position and overlooking almost all of the land in the lower part of the estate.

The Manor Pound was, and still is, below the house, and the Manor Mill only a few hundred yards down the street. When the men of the town went to the Butt Garden for their archery practice, as they were obliged to do in the time of Henry VIII, they could be watched by the Lord or his Bailiff from the windows of the house. (The Butt Garden was a meadow near the present Fire Station.)

In about 1840 Mr Blathwayt, the then Lord of the Manor, decided to build a new road, intended as a scenic drive rather than an attempt to avoid Porlock Hill. This started from just above the Ship Inn, and followed an easier gradient for four and a half miles to

Pitt Combe Head. It was dug out manually, no doubt providing valuable work during the depressed times after the Napoleonic Wars. Mr Blathwayt went out in a boat with a fisherman from Porlock Weir to view and plan the course of the road. He employed a French engineer. The route needed several bridges over, and culverts under, the steep coombes, and much excavation. It cut through existing stone walls where tenants' lands were divided, and also field walls. It also cut through the old track from Porlockford to Birchanger Farm.

At first the road was just a rough track used by horses. One wonders what Mr Blathwayt would have made of motor cars using it, let alone lorries and motor coaches.

The earliest toll list which has been found is:

Porlock New Road. Turnpike accounts:

List of charges; August 12th., 1857	s.	d.
Horse and Gig		6
Horse and Cart		4
Carriage and 2 horses	1	0
Carriage and pair	1	0
Coach	1	6
Horse		1
Wagon		9
Donkey		3
Bus and 4 horses	1	6
Machine and 3 horses		9
Engine and 3 horses		9

It is interesting to see that a donkey was three-pence whereas a horse was only a penny. It can only be assumed that a donkey carried a load and a horse was usually used for pleasure, or perhaps to carry a farmer home or out on business.

Pine trees were planted and are still to be seen marking the line of the road. Chestnut and walnut trees were planted amongst the natural oak and ash, and there were later various conifer

Court Place Farm.

Painting by John Phelps, 1836, showing the Old Town, Mill and Castle Inn.

plantations. From time to time these have been felled and replanted.

The first tolls were taken at the Ship Inn. There used to be a gate across at the bottom of the road, opposite the

One of the hairpin bends on the Porlock Toll Road.

View of the village c1900, showing the Tannery buildings on the left.

present Village Hall. In quiet times a boy would run out from the Ship Inn to take the toll, but on busy days in summer time, or on a hunting day, he would stay at the gate.

In 1924 the Toll Houses were built at the halfway point and the gate at Porlock was taken away. The stone for the houses came partly from the Keeper's Cottage, about a quarter of a mile from the site, at the top of the wood above Aller Park. There is little to be seen there now except the garden wall and part of the floor of the cottage. There is one odd window of leaded glass in one of the Toll Cottages, which came from the Keeper's Cottage.

With the advent of the motor car, the road came to be very much used. Many people today prefer to pay a toll rather than risk Porlock Hill. In my younger days everyone referred to the road as the New Road rather than the Toll Road. The New Road has been a great asset to Porlock, as it also makes a lovely walk, especially at quiet times. The scenery for walker and motorist alike, especially on the downward journey, makes it one of the most beautiful routes in the area.

16

WEST PORLOCK

THE ROAD FROM Porlock to the harbour at Porlock Weir passes through the hamlet of West Porlock. West Porlock House, now divided into two, with bungalows in the grounds, was the Manor House built by the Blathwayt family in the 1920s. It was not used very much as a family residence as their main house and estate was at Dyrham Park. The building material for the house was stone taken from a small quarry in the wood near the house, and some other type of stone brought by boat to Porlock Weir.

There are some lovely old cottages, many of them modernised but retaining old features. During the restoration of one old cottage, the door needed to be replaced; this was unfortunate because the old one was very interesting. Roughly carved into it was a heart with an arrow through it. This is believed to have been a sign to ward off witches.

During alterations at Dunns Court, near the centre of the hamlet, two lovely inglenook fireplaces were opened up, as well as an old faggot oven. A hiding place for valuables was found in the stone floor, where a mat would have covered it. The outbuildings had stalls for carthorses, because it was the Manor Farm at one time.

At the top of the steep on the left is a large cottage known as Fern Cottage, part of an old house which some time in the last century was used as a public house called the Live and Let Live. The last landlady was a Mrs Burgess. Her descendants

West Porlock, c1910.

Top of West Porlock Steep with the Live and Let Live in the centre.

have told me that it was an alehouse: the old lady had a licence to sell only ale. The authorities found out that she was selling spirits as well and consequently she lost her licence. One wonders whether the spirits were obtained legally, or smuggled in.

Mr Moggridge the blacksmith at his forge, c1900.

The lock-up and the old forge (converted into a dwelling c.1950), 2009.

Our strip of coast was no different from the rest of the coast of England during the 17th and 18th centuries, when taxes on imports were so high that many people thought smuggling a fair game.

The Cook family, who lived at the Live and Let Live in my memory, had, for two generations, collected ferns which were gathered, under a licence from both the Blathwayt and Lovelace families, from the Parks and Culbone Woods. The ferns, which were true ferns, not bracken, were made up into circular bundles, carefully laid with the stalks outwards. The bundles were then covered in hessian. The carrier would pick them up and take them to Minehead station, from where they would be sent to London by train. They were sold to the fish-markets for displaying fish on the marble slabs. Fishmongers still use ferns, but they are not real, only plastic!

Further along the road is the old forge, now cleverly converted into a private dwelling. The last blacksmith was Mr Jack Moggridge, who followed his father at the forge. The usual smithing jobs were carried out there, including shoeing. There in the yard is a little thatched building, where Mr Moggridge used to keep his cider; it was originally the village lock-up. Tradition has it, although there is no written record, that it was used by the village constable to lock up suspected rebels in the Monmouth Rebellion pending transfer to Judge Jeffrey's Assizes; and also, later on, seamen captured from the French and Spanish privateers.

At the west end of the hamlet, the last cottage on the left has a large leaded window. This was the little shop and workshop of the leather craftsman, Mr Philip Burgess.

Earlier he was in the building trade. It was Mr Burgess who re-shingled the church steeple in 1890, and fixed up a little platform which could be hauled up and down to work from. He learnt how to do embossed leather work in a class for boys started by a Miss Baker at Chapel Knap. He became so good at this work that he eventually set up in business. Some of his work can be seen in the area, notably the angels on the reredos in Selworthy Church, and a frieze showing a hunting scene around a room at New Place, built by Sir Charles Chadwyck-Healey.

On one occasion a gentleman called at his shop and, looking around, became interested in his work. He asked if Mr Burgess could copy an old worn leather seat. A few days later the chair cover arrived. The pattern was so worn that it was difficult to follow. Mr Burgess put a lot of time and trouble into this work and, when it was finished, he sent it, together with the old cover, to the address given, somewhere in the City of London. At last a letter came in response. There was a good cheque inside and the gentleman had written: 'We have examined your work alongside the original and are unanimously of the opinion it is the better work of the two. The old piece was taken from a

Philip Burgess's leather shop on the right, c1920.

chair in the chancel of St Paul's Cathedral. Yours is now in its place, and I hope will remain there for some hundreds of years.'

Between West Porlock and Porlockford there was once an orchard known as Gaptree Orchard. The Gaptree was blown down during the 1950s and fell across the road. This spot was said to be haunted by the ghost of Nelly Carew. She was a character in *Katerfelto*, a novel by G.J. Whyte-Melville. He stayed for a time at Porlockford and soaked up the atmosphere of the Porlock area. In this novel he well describes the life and scenery of Porlock Bay and Exmoor. Although not as well-known as R.D. Blackmore's *Lorna Doone*, it is nevertheless a very good novel.

Porlockford House was built on the site of a previous house and has been a riding centre for many years. The ford, of course, is now bridged where the stream flows under the road near the entrance to the house.

Just a short way up into the woods the Village Hut is situated. It has always been known as The Hut, but it used to be much used by the residents of Porlock Weir and West Porlock for social events such as dances and meetings. It was originally an Army building from the First World War and it is still in use.

17

PORLOCK WEIR

PORLOCK WEIR has been essential to the economy of Porlock for centuries. We can only surmise that the first harbour had been built by the 15th century as the Bailiff of Brendon's accounts of 1422-3 include an item 'paid to Robert Godde [the lady's receiver] for the repair of the Weir at West Porlock'; and, in 1426: '1 heifer paid to Robert Godde – clerk – for the making of the Weir at Porlock.' The name *Weir* puzzles people as there is no sizable river, and no weir on it. There are other meanings of the word, however: it can be a fishing weir, where posts were fixed at low water level to hold nets for trapping fish, possibly salmon. R.D. Blackmore in *Lorna Doone* refers to Lynmouth Weir, and we know that this method of fishing has been used along the Bristol Channel coast for years. A weir is also a place for building boats, and for careening the hulls (scraping off the barnacles). Some believe that Worthy Water once entered the harbour but made a new course after a severe flood many years ago.

On the harbour wall, c1910.

The first harbour would have been quite crude, and early photographs and the Ordnance Survey map of 1888 show a bridge further up the dock than at present. Records show that money was spent from time to time on the dock and lock gates. The lock gates, which replaced the previous wooden ones, were erected in about 1913, and were constructed away from Porlock. There are similar ones in the old docks at Cardiff.

There was an official opening of the new dock, when all the local people turned out. Bunting decorated the boats known as trows, which are mainly used on the River Severn and the upper reaches of the Channel.

At one time quite sizable vessels, up to one hundred tons, came into Porlock Weir – men would have to slide back the bridge by pulling on ropes.

Sluice tunnel and sluice house above, c1930.

As a boy I often watched the unloading of coal: a pulley worked by a donkey engine in the vessel was used. The coal was lifted from the hold in maunds (double handled wicker baskets). Much of the coal was stored in the yard and sheds behind the harbour house, now Pieces of Eight, from where it was delivered by horse and cart, and later by lorries. In 1875 there was also a brick and tile company beside the inner harbour.

There used to be several fishing families: I remember Preston and Arthur Ley, and Jack Ridler, who had

Porlock Weir harbour and Turkey Cottages, 2008 – now all pleasure craft.

The inner harbour at Porlock Weir, c1900. Note the footbridge to Turkey Cottages and the old lock gates.

fishing boats. Before them there were the Pugsley and Pollard Brothers, and Perkins, and Mr Ward. Often I have seen Preston Ley out in the bay on a cold winter's day fishing with drift nets for herring.

Porlock Weir herrings were very popular, being much fresher than those brought down from Great Yarmouth. There are several reasons why the herrings have declined in number in the Bristol Channel: over-fishing in the Channel approaches and pollution are just two. For hundreds of years boats went out for herrings from Minehead, Porlock Weir, Lynmouth and other parts of North Devon. The fish would be sold from the quays and local shops, or delivered by dealers around the villages and farms. When there were plenty, some would be salted down in barrels. (The saltern at Porlock Weir was later a carpenter's workshop). If there was still a surplus, it was known for the fish to be sent to Bossington for spreading on the land as fertilizer.

The fish market at Porlock Weir, to be seen in early photographs, was situated opposite the Anchor Hotel, on the edge of the present car park; it was just a fenced-in area. Here the fishermen sold their catch until the turn of the 20th century. The herrings were in maunds or boxes, and whilst the joulers (the dealers) were haggling over the price, the men would be 'telling up the catch'. Herrings were sold in long hundreds, and the method of counting was thus: two men would count out in threes; each would pick up three herrings in turn and count, 'Wan, two, dree' and so on, up to forty – that is 120 herrings. Then at the next three the men would say, 'Warp and tail,' and one herring would be placed on the ground. Then the counting would be repeated as many times as necessary until the buyer had enough long hundreds. The one on the ground representing each long hundred could easily be counted; for example, if there were five herrings on the ground,

The ketch Mistletoe *of Porlock Weir on 15th September 1913, celebrating the reopening of the harbour with the new lock gates.*

The inner harbour, c1960.

there were five long hundred in the buyer's box or basket. Therefore it was easy to keep count. The three herrings for 'warp and tail' were extra, I am told, to cover any turnpike tolls on the buyer's journey. When herrings were plentiful at that time they were sold for 2/6d a hundred.

At the point where the lower road from Porlock begins its run alongside the beach is the site of the former barkhouse. Trees were felled and stripped in the woods, and the bark stored here for transporting to the Tannery in Porlock. There were more fields on the seaward side of the barkshed, but they were gradually swept away by erosion; the road itself is preserved by the massive concrete walling on either side of the steps leading down to the beach.

The old map of Porlock in the Museum dated about 1710 shows an oyster bed in Porlock Bay. Oysters were dredged for many years on both sides of the Channel. Perhaps the fishing went on for some years after that map was produced. Noah and William Pollard's uncle and his crew were dredging for oysters off Mumbles in about 1870, but with little success; returning to Porlock, they decided to try their luck once more in Porlock Bay. To their astonishment they made a wonderful catch, and so decided to continue oyster fishing. They were catching an average of twelve hundred per day. The dredge was towed behind their sailing boat on a long line. It had a cutting edge of iron about one metre long, known as the sword. The oysters were dragged off the sea bottom into a type of net made of chain link. The net would be hauled up and tipped into the boat. The oysters were then kept in a walled-in area known as a perch, where the tides left them at low water. They remained in the perch in bags of six hundred, until needed. Most of the oysters were sent to Bristol.

The oyster perch remains at Porlock Weir, right opposite the two houses built for William and Noah Pollard named Oyster Perch and Mizpah (the second a biblical name meaning watchtower). Whether there are still oysters in Porlock Bay is debatable as the waters are very polluted nowadays. It used to be said that the oyster fishing finished when boats from the East Coast, from Whitstable and Colchester, came and dredged the oyster beds in order to replenish their stocks. As there was no law to prevent this, all the Pollard brothers could do was look helplessly on.

The brothers Pollard were not only fishermen but boat-builders too. The indentures of Noah Pollard are still held by his family. Boats had been built at Porlock Weir for a long time; in 1723 there was a charge of '3 shillings upon every boat, and 6 shillings on every barque built upon the lords waste'.

There was also a very comprehensive list of tolls payable to Mr William Blathwayt, the then Lord. This gave the harbour dues for imports and exports of 78 different commodities as varied as fish, fruit and – at a charge of one penny for every dozen pairs – stockings.

In more recent times many a boat was laid up and left to rot in the inner harbour during the depression that followed the First World War. Many boats were converted into pleasure cruisers; one, the *Breeze*, lay beside the dock for many years and was seldom used. The *Breeze* was formerly a Bristol Channel Pilot Cutter of nineteen tons. Built in 1887 at Pill, she is the last of the Transom Stern Pilot Cutters. *Breeze* has now been taken to a barn at Bossington Farm, where it is hoped that she may one day be restored.

Just after the Second World War Porlock Weir formed a Sailing Club which ran very successfully for several years. Some members obtained new eighteen-foot sailing dinghies, some designed and built by Uffa Fox of Cowes fame, and some from Kimbers' yard at Highbridge. Porlock Weir boats competed in many of the Bristol Channel races off Mumbles, Barry and Weston. The Club, disbanded for a number of years, has now reformed.

Boat trips around the bay were once very popular, and provided extra income, in addition to fishing trips, when the herring season had finished. Some fishermen's wives let rooms for boarding or bed and breakfast. Some served teas, or made up trays of tea for visitors to take to the beach. Sea swimming was very popular when the weather was good, and water polo was played in the harbour for a few seasons.

The three hotels have also been kept busy, especially since the great increase in motor traffic. Although the people who used to take rooms for the hunting season no longer do so, the stables are gradually being converted to other uses, or incorporated into hotel use.

At the turn of the 20th century the Landlord at the Anchor Hotel was Mr James Goddard. The hotel was mainly used by guests who were there for the hunting season. Mr Goddard kept up to twenty-five horses. He also ran a horse bus to carry passengers from and to the station at Minehead for a fare of 1/6d. Porlock Weir was always an attraction at high tides, and even more so when there were very high tides in September. I have seen the yard of the Ship Inn full of sea water and once watched the landlord, Bernard Perkins, watch in hand, standing at the door of the bar. The water was already lapping the step, but he didn't even put a sandbag across it. He knew the time of the

The washout at Porlock Weir, December 1910.
Was it a tsunami?

tide, and, sure enough, within a few minutes the water had started to recede.

That was a fairly quiet evening tide, but there are occasions when some of the cottages get flooded. There was the famous time in 1910, which

Damage done at Porlock Weir after the great storm of December 1910.
The sea washed away the garden walls and most of the gardens
at Oyster Perch and Mizpah.

The beach continually shifts at Porlock Weir, necessitating the making of groins or timber hedges. The harbour used to be sluiced through a tunnel, not now used; the sluice was controlled from a stone building on the quay. The lock gates would be closed and then opened for sluicing, but this was not very satisfactory because the flow of water went in too much of an easterly direction. Sometimes a mechanical digger is used.

At Porlockford the sea has encroached on the land considerably and the sea wall had to be strengthened early in the 1950s. Before the reservoir was built along the Toll Road, the Porlock Weir water supply came from a stream flowing through a culvert all the way from Steart Bridge, below Birchanger Farm.

The harbour was small and could accommodate only small vessels. One top-sail schooner, the *Florence Muspratt* of 78 tons, was owned by Mr Harry Manley during the First World War. Mr Manley kept the grocer's shop at the Weir. The ship had too great a draught to enter the harbour, but did trade up and down the Channel and beyond. As she sailed past Porlock Weir, Mr Manley would point her out with pride, and she always dipped her ensign on passing her owner's port. The vessel was built at Burton Struther in

folk talked about for many years, referring to a tidal wave or the 'wash out' at Porlock Weir. On that occasion much damage was done. The road leading to the village was covered in stones. The hedge on the other side of the road was partially washed away and the sea came halfway up the gardens of Oyster Perch and Mizpah. The cottages at Gibraltar, which back onto the beach, were all flooded. A Miss Pugsley was to be married and her wedding cake was on the sitting-room table; both table and cake floated to the ceiling, and were then submerged in sea water. Mr Stenner, the baker, quickly replaced the cake. Everyone had to spend the night in the Church at the top of Lane Head. There was considerable structural damage to the houses.

Jim Sparkes, who was a boy at the time, nearly lost his life when a wave swept into the bedroom at Beach Cottage and, on receding, dragged him to the bedroom window. He had a lucky escape, as Mr Pollard caught him and held him.

Lincolnshire in 1869. She was commandeered for war service in 1914. On September 5th 1917, whilst under the command of Captain Jack Redd, she sailed from St Malo for Newport in ballast, to pick up coal. Unfortunately she was fired on by a German submarine. One member of the crew was killed; the captain and two others took to the boat, but a few minutes later she sank. The surviving crew were luckily picked up by a French patrol boat, and they returned by cross-channel ferry to Southampton. On September 12th they reached Minehead by train.

Other schooners, *The Flying Foam* of 85 tons and the *Periton*, traded with France and sometimes with the Mediterranean countries and the Azores. The *Periton* sank without loss of life when she was run down by another ship on a voyage to Ireland. This ship was so named because she was built at Minehead in 1887 from oak timbers and larch board hewn from Periton Wood. She is believed to have been the only ship launched from Minehead.

Another of the Porlock Weir craft was the *Fanny*, built at Aberthaw in 1753. She was first owned by John Moore, and then several generations of the Pulsford family. She traded between South Wales and Minehead, and was wrecked at Barry in 1883. William

Worthy and Ashley Combe House, home of the Lovelace family, c1920.

Pulsford built his own smack, the *John and William*, at the back of the harbour in 1858, and the Pollard brothers built the *Rosa*. Then there were William Pollard's *Two Sisters*, John Perkins' *Betsy*, John Red's *Caerleon*.

Later Tom Ley came from Coombe Martin with his *Mistletoe* and settled at Porlock Weir, where his sons, grandsons and great-grandson carried on the tradition of small-boat fishing. My own memories are of coal boats such as the *Bessie Clarke* and the *Democrat* of Barnstaple, which sank off the French coast.

During the 19th century many of the cargoes were culm from Swansea, coal from Penarth and limestone from Barry; other imports were salt, flour and groceries. Pit props were the main export, to South Wales and Bristol; also brick cargoes to Bristol and, in summer, brick and bark to Penzance.

Beyond Porlock Weir is Worthy, a lovely house, parts of which are very old. We know there was a house at Worthy as early as the reign of Edward I. The estate, which once consisted of a farm and about forty acres of land, was frequently called Worthy Manor, but there is no evidence that it was ever entitled to be described as a manor in the correct sense. As the house is small, it was no doubt a part of Porlock Manor, and it is still just within the boundary.

Ashley Combe House, c1900.

In the woods above Worthy, and on the far side of the combe, are the ruins of Ashley Combe House, formerly known as Ashley Combe Lodge, which was demolished in the 1960s. It is believed that a house was on the site in the 17th century. It was Lord King, the 8th Baron (later to become the first Lord Lovelace) who improved and extended the property and created the Italian Gardens. The house was built in the style of an Italian chateau, and there were several tunnels in the grounds large enough for traders' vehicles to approach the house. Many trees were planted in the grounds. The Lovelace family owned Yearnor, Culbone, Sparkhayes and Bratton near Minehead. The view from the house was magnificent, looking over Porlock Weir and across the bay.

Lord King married Ada, the daughter of Lord Byron. Countess Ada Lovelace is one of the few women to figure in computing history. She was a gifted mathematician who understood Charles Babbage's analytical engine and wrote some of the best accounts of how it worked. She even devised programs for it: she was thus the world's first computer programmer.

Babbage first invented the difference engine, the first calculator, in 1822; the analytical engine, which he designed in 1834, could handle up to eighty digits and included many of the features of the modern computer. The programs were controlled from punched cards and results were printed automatically. The government of the day, who were impressed by the invention, granted him £1,500, which later grew to £17,000 (equal to £1,700,000 today).

The Porlock Weir fishermen used to take visitors out for boat trips on fine summer days. One trip to Rockford Cottage was advertised as to a 'Smuggler's cottage'. It lay about a quarter of a mile beyond Gore Point. It was really a boathouse, from which a path led up through the woods to Ashley Combe House. The access from the beach would have been ideal for smuggling, but I would hesitate to say that that was its purpose. Unfortunately the path and almost all of the cottage have now disappeared due to continuous landslips in the Culbone Woods.

I wonder whether Porlock Weir people saw the French ships coming up the Channel in 1797 with a force, many of whom were released convicts, intending to land at Bristol and march on London. The ships had been sighted off Ilfracombe, where an old lady had stood on the cliff beating a kettledrum as a warning. However, when in sight of Porlock, the wind was contrary, so the invaders turned and sailed down-Channel and around St David's head to land at Fishguard, where they were soon rounded up by the inhabitants and the Castle Martin yeomanry.

18
FLOODING

The Exmoor area with its steep hills is very prone to sudden flooding during heavy rains. Some will recall the Lynmouth flood of August 15th 1952. This storm also affected Porlock in a smaller way. Several houses were flooded and the Hawkcombe road washed out quite badly at Higher Hawkcombe. Money from the flood fund was made available and used to tar the road for the first time from just above Sunnyside to above Peep Out.

There have also been flash floods in the summer time, usually during thunderstorms, but the worst flood in recent years was in October 1960, when the Hawkcombe Stream was blocked under the culvert of the bridge in the main street. The result was that the water came down Hawkcombe and Parson Street, flooding many shops and houses to a depth of up to four feet. The camp field in Sparkhayes was like a lake with a waterfall coming off the field into Sparkhayes at the end of Furzeland Road. The water flowed like a river about three feet deep

Water coming off a field on to Sparkhayes Lane, 1960.

down Sparkhayes Lane to the Marsh. The sewer pipe which ran down the lane, and had been laid early in the 20th century, was left completely exposed, and the stones which had been washed out of the trench were deposited at the bottom of the lane. A new sewer was laid afterwards across the fields, parallel with the old sewer.

The culvert under the bridge was cleared, and the river widened where possible, with walls built beside the river in Hawkcombe. The type of floods described here had been happening from time to time over many years.

Porlock Marsh in the 1960s. It was used in the summer time for grazing horses, cattle and sheep. The beginning of the Porlock Parks can be seen on the right.

Coy Barn on Porlock Marsh. Note how all the trees have died due to the salt water from the high tide.

A man who lived at Porlock Weir once told me that the Worthy Stream used to run into Porlock Weir harbour, but during a great storm it broke through to make a new outlet to the sea, where it still is. The story was probably passed on for generations. It is on record that on October 13th

1625 there was a great flood, and it is also recorded that a number of persons made a petition to Quarter Sessions at Wells on July 11th 1626. It was signed by two Magistrates, the Minister and twenty-seven residents of Porlock. The victim of this flood was 'Grace Moggridge of Porlock, Widow, whose house and grounds were lying neare the sea by a small lake, whose discent is from a very steepe woodie mountayne.' It is most likely that this was at the foot of Worthy Combe. It appears that poor Grace Moggridge's dwelling house, outhouses, fishing equipment, garden and two acres of orchard and hops etc were washed into the sea, the total cost of the damage being £200 and upwards. It was decided at the sessions to advance 'the poor woman £6 13s 4d towards her relief in this her extremitie'.

Other big floods caused by high tides coinciding with high winds occurred in 1859, when a hundred sheep drowned on Porlock Marsh, and in 1910, when the new Golf Course was washed away.

More recently, in 1983 sixty-three sheep were drowned, and in the spring of 1990 two large breaches were made in the pebble ridge, moving hundreds of tons of boulders and shingle, and flooding the marsh and lower fields. This storm was the worst in the memory of many Porlock folk.

Hawkcombe Stream overflowed and the culvert was blocked, resulting in the road being gouged out and the sewer pipe broken, 1960.

The road washed out near Mill Cottages, 1960.

19
SOME VILLAGE CHARACTERS

MANY PEOPLE from the cities and towns used to look on the countryman as a bit of a yokel, even as uneducated. But this was not so. Many youngsters who grew up in the villages or on farms reached high positions in later life.

For example, Ernest Bevin, the wartime Cabinet Minister, came from Winsford; George Williams, who founded the YMCA, was born on a farm near Dulverton. And, prior to this, there were many famous people who came from the West Country. Many young people who left Porlock rose in rank in their careers – in the police, the Army and Navy, as well as in the business and industrial world.

Many others stayed in Porlock and expanded their own businesses. Quite a number moved into Minehead, where there was more scope with the growing population and the tourist trade. Several of the larger Minehead businesses were started by men from Porlock. Those who did stay on, and who spent their working days in the village, often showed that they had had a good grounding at the village school, and perhaps later at Minehead, Taunton or Wellington schools. Amongst older men who hadn't had such a good chance, perhaps having left school at fourteen or even twelve years old, there were those who, despite their lack of education, were still intelligent and witty. Those who were not very literate were often the butt of other people's tricks – as always, there were those who lived by their wits.

Here are a few amusing stories about the characters who lived in Porlock and the surrounding villages.

Mr Bill Court used to drive a horse and cart for Cooksleys the Builders. One of his regular jobs was bringing up stones from Bossington Beach. One day he got to the bottom of Bush Steep, on his way to Porlock, and met two gentlemen who were on holiday from London. One of them, I suspect, thought, 'Here's a countryman we can have some fun with!' So he said, 'Excuse me, my man! Have you seen a cartload of monkeys passing this way?' Mr Court scratched his head in thought, then he said, 'No sir, why? 'Ave you two fell off?' The visitors were so taken aback by this quick-witted reply that one asked Mr Court, 'Which pub do you patronise?' – to which the reply was 'The Royal Oak.' The result, of course, was a free drink or two that evening.

In the bar of the Ship Inn at Porlock Weir a holiday-maker asked one of the locals, Bob Davis, 'What do you do here to pass the time during the winter when all the visitors have gone home?' 'Oh,' says Bob, 'we 'aves a lovely time, we just sits yer and laughs and laughs and laughs.' 'Good Lord,' says the visitor, 'whatever do you laugh about?' 'Why, sir,' says Bob, 'we laughs at all you silly b—s that come down yer in the summer.'

Bob Davis was a very clever man with his hands. He lived in a little cottage at Porlock Weir which is now named Bob's Cottage. Although he could barely read or write he was very good at repairing clocks. His little room was full of them. He could also true-up a buckled bicycle wheel. He made wooden furniture, and sails for a boat; he even made a violin once, and played it. It is said he once made a boat in his house but couldn't get it through the door, so he had to break it up again. I was once talking to another Porlock character, Charlie Powell, and I said that Bob Davis was a very clever man. 'Oh yes,' says Charlie, 'Bob Davis is a well educated man, but it's a pity he can't read or write.'

Charlie used to blow the Church organ when Mr Sidney Cooksley was the organist. One Sunday Charlie said, 'You can play what you like, Mr Cooksley, I'm going to blow for "Rock of Ages".'

Another story concerning Charlie I heard only recently. It came from a man who sang in the Church choir when he was a boy. The boys collected about twenty snails from the churchyard and put them on Charlie's seat by the organ. They hoped to have a laugh, but fortunately for Charlie the organist came first, and, wanting to change his shoes, sat on the snails himself.

Of course, some stories are true and can be vouched for while others are somewhat far fetched. They get embellished by better storytellers, so you need to take some of the stories with a pinch of salt.

One story was first told during the last war. White lines were painted in the middle of the road so that drivers could keep to the road during the blackout. Some found that the best way to drive was to straddle the line; when they saw another light approaching they would move to the left. Remember there was nothing like the amount of traffic that there is today. One night a Porlock resident drove home from Minehead, following the white line intently until he could go no further: he had arrived at the posts in the road outside the Anchor Hotel at Porlock Weir without realising he'd driven straight through Porlock.

There were, of course, always practical jokers up to tricks for the fun of it. Young lads would often be sent on errands with notes asking the receiver to send them on further. Or they'd be

Johnny Floyd's donkey cart, the local taxi, c1900.

Three ladies walking past Myrtle Cottage towards Red Rose Cottage on the right, c1900.

sent to the leather shop for strap oil and be given a slap with a leather strap. Schoolboys would tie two door knockers together and knock on one door; when it was answered the other knocker would lift – and so it would go on.

One day at West Porlock the boys put a sack of bricks over the chimney of the blacksmith's shop. Of course, the shop became very smoky and Jack Moggridge, the blacksmith, said, 'Phew, smoke's flying low, there must be rain about.' When he realised that the chimney was blocked he poked a rod up it and dislodged the sack, which came down through the roof.

An old lady, Lizzie Jarvis, lived in a cottage next to the school playground. The boys would throw stones from the playground and try to get them down her chimney. One day she went into the school to complain with two stones in her frying pan.

There was a man called Jim Pulsford at Porlock Weir, and people said he was a 'proper scamp'. This was what they used to call someone who was worse than the average practical joker. One day a lady who lived at Worthy Manor lost one of her peacocks and offered a reward to anyone who found it. Jim Pugsley was working in the woods above Worthy and from the other side of the combe Jim Pulsford saw him catch the lost peacock. Quick as a flash Jim Pulsford went down and knocked on the door of Worthy Manor and said to the lady, 'It's all right Ma'am, we've caught the peacock. Jim Pugsley will be bringing him down in a few minutes.' 'Oh, thank you,' said the lady, 'here's your reward.' Off went Pulsford with the money.

On another occasion Pulsford again went off with the money. He took a party of chaps carol singing to Ashley Combe. There was at that time a regular Village Choir led by 'Tinker' Huish, the Porlock blacksmith. They used to go round the district each year, and were known as Tinker's Choir. Pulsford got to Ashley Combe, where his choir sang for a few minutes. Lady Lovelace came out and asked them if they were Tinker's Choir. 'Oh yes,' said Pulsford. So she gave them the money and off they went. It can be imagined what was said when later the real Tinker's Choir turned up at Ashley Combe and began to sing.

The mode of speech was very different among village people even when I was a boy. One day I was sent with a pair of bellows for repair to Tinker Huish. Several days later I met him in the Drang and he said, 'Yer, I've mend thee bellas.' 'Pardon?' I said. 'I've mend thee bellas,' he repeated. Three times he said it before I understood what he meant!

Mr Isaac Burgess was delivering bread to the Ship Inn at Porlock when a certain man who had recently taken up preaching in the Methodist Church was in the bar having a drink. On seeing Mr Burgess approaching, and knowing that he was not only a keen Methodist but also a teetotaler (not all were), the man asked William Rook, the landlord, 'What shall I do, Mr Rook'. 'Hide in that cupboard,' said Mr Rook. So the man stepped inside the cupboard. Mr Burgess entered and asked how much bread. 'A couple of loaves,' said Mr Rook. 'Put them in that cupboard there, don't leave them on the bar.' Whereupon Mr Burgess opened the cupboard door, and there was the nameless gentleman inside with a glass of beer in his hand.

Until a few years ago there were two bakers in the village, Burgess's and Stenner's. This story concerns Mr Walter Stenner who used to call at a house with a very large family from whom he was having difficulty getting his money. One day he called with the bread; after putting it on the table, the daughter of the house said, 'Mother can't pay today, she's gone to Minehead.' 'Oh?' said Mr Stenner. 'Next time she goes, tell her to take her feet with her.' The lady had hidden behind a curtain and the toes of her shoes were showing underneath.

A Porlock lady used to tell a tale of a man who was a local preacher, who went to preach at Wheddon Cross before there was a Chapel there. He stood on top of a barrel to preach and, being rather a ranter, he started to get excited and began to shout: 'The righteous shall rise up, and the wicked shall go down to hell!' – wherewith the top of the barrel caved in and down he went.

Old Charlie went up to Hacketty Way House and asked Mr Fairchild, the head gardener, for some bedding plants. 'How many do you want, Charlie?' asked Mr Fairchild. 'Oh, only two or three,' says Charlie, 'but mix 'em up a bit, will 'ee?'

Children get strange ideas. At Porlock School some children were discussing the 'Trow Pool' which is opposite the Anchor Hotel at Porlock Weir. A boy who lived at Porlock Weir said it was bottomless; he knew it was bottomless because his father had helped to dig it!

Another young boy from Porlock Weir went to sea in a local ketch. Of course his father was very proud of him. When asked how the boy was getting on, he said, 'He's doing very well, he's been to foreign parts.' 'Foreign parts?' was the question. 'Oh 'ees, Lynmouth and Cardiff and about.'

A chimney sweep sweeping a chimney at the Anchor Hotel asked Jim Pulsford to give him a shout when the brush came out at the top. He kept putting on more rods and shouting to Jim, asking if the brush was up. 'No,' said Jim, so more rods were put on. 'Not up yet,' shouted Jim. Still more rods were put on. The sweep couldn't understand why Jim hadn't shouted! So he called again to Jim. When there was no reply he went outside. Jim had disappeared and the brush was hanging down over the roof nearly to the road.

Some young men played a joke one night, hanging up a horn lantern from the flagpole outside the Anchor Hotel at Porlock Weir. Two old chaps came out of the Ship Inn, having had a drop too much. One looked up at the light, 'Caw, I've never seen the moon looking so dirty!' 'No,' said the other, 'and I've never seen 'en out north before!'

One day I learned that a shark had been washed up on the beach at Porlock Weir. When I saw my friend Ernie Pollard I said, 'I hear there's a shark at Porlock Weir.' Quick as a flash, he laughed as he replied, 'Ah, and I reckon there's a few up Porlock too.'

When Mr Goddard kept the Anchor Hotel at the end of the 19th century he had a scarecrow made and put up in one of the fields at the back of the hotel. One local man who went up there thought that the clothes on the scarecrow were

View towards Parsons Hill before electric lights, c1914.
There is an oil lamp outside the Chapel.

View towards Parsons Hill showing the Porlock Café,
formerly the Wesleyan Chapel, c1950.

better than his own, so he changed clothes with it and went on his way.

Sometimes, in excitement, words are put the wrong way round. A man at Luccombe one day saw a lady repairing her fence. She was not making a very good job of it, so he offered to help. 'Don't worry missus,' he said. 'Give us half a dozen hammers and a nail, and I'll soon mend thee fence.'

Ted Kent, an undertaker who lived at Allerford, went to visit a friend on Selworthy Green who was ill. Whilst there he said to his friend, 'Well I may as well run the tape over 'ee while I'm yer!'

The same man took a party of carol singers out one Christmas and they sang at the home of the Stenner family who kept the Allerford Laundry at Brandish Street (now demolished). When they had sung a few carols they were invited inside for refreshments. Miss Stenner handed round some mince pies, which everyone enjoyed, so Mr Kent said, 'Nice mince pies, Miss Stenner.' And, turning to his friends, he said, 'Would you chaps like some more?' Miss Stenner was obliged to bring out more.

Trying to take ourselves back and visualise what life was like in the past, how it differed from today, is not easy. For example, we are used to seeing all the summer traffic and tourists today. I was told this next story by Mr Arthur Smith, who at one time had a shoemaker's shop and business at Doverhay, next to the present car park. An old uncle of his, Mr Jim Sparks, who lived at the top of Villes Lane, was sitting on a wall outside his home watching the traffic go by. It was the day of the opening meet in August 1910. Having counted 63 cars going towards Lynmouth, and 61 coming back, he said, 'I don't know whatever 'tis coming to.' What would he say if he could see how many cars pass through towards Lynmouth today?

The first car in Porlock was a second-hand Peugeot, the second a 1903 Wolseley, both owned by Mr Pearce the tanner. Mr Frank Pocock, his chauffeur, went to Birmingham to await the completion of the Wolseley, and then drove it back to Porlock. Mr Pearce's granddaughter, Miss Joan Pearce, told me that she had ridden in it as a little girl, and laughingly told me that when it rained they had put up their umbrellas.

There was an old lady in Porlock who was always on the lookout for anything she could pick up. The boys would play her up. They would drop a handkerchief attached to a long piece of string and watch her pick it up and, thinking no one was looking, tuck it under her knicker elastic. The boys would wait just long enough and then give the string a tug, so the handkerchief was pulled out. The same old lady was seen coming out of the door to the Rectory garden. As she came out a heap of apples fell out of her knickers.

Tom Webber was a character who earned his living by picking primroses and whortleberries and selling them during the spring and summer. In the winter he chopped sticks and sold bundles for firelighting, and also did odd jobs, especially for sympathetic elderly ladies who could afford to pay him. He lived with his sister and a brother, and every evening he could be seen at his bedroom window counting his money, which he was always talking about. It was a fact that he did have money invested, but he always exaggerated how much he had. He told me that he had money in 'fower' banks. If he talked of so many thousand, he was referring to shillings not pounds!

One of my Grandfather's customers was a Mrs Fowler at West Porlock. She had a large family and had got behind with her payments. One day she offered him a ham which had been cured and was hanging in the chimneyplace. When Mr Fowler returned, he said to his wife, 'Wa's thee done with thic there ham?' Mrs Fowler replied, 'I've given 'en to Isaac Burgess to pay the bread bill.' 'Well,' said Mr Fowler, 'thee tell Isaac Burgess to bring thic there ham back again.'

Talking of food, someone who lived in Hawkcombe, when eating his rabbit stew, declared that the best part of a rabbit stew was the dough boys (dumplings).

A popular activity about a century ago was bird-batting. Men would go out at night with a long net on two poles and stretch it over a hedge. One would hold a lantern behind the net while others walked along the other side, beating the hedge with sticks. The roosting birds would fly out towards the light and get caught in the net, and eventually finish up in a pie. Once my Grandmother told me that she had blackbird pie when she was a young girl, but I also remember her telling me off because I'd taken a black-bird's egg from the nest. How quickly attitudes change.

A Porlock man appeared before the Bench at Dunster Police Court to give evidence in a murder case. The Magistrate asked him his name, and then his occupation. 'A tailor, sir,' was the reply, "'an' I could clap a patch on the ass of your trousers, as good as any man.'

There was a small farm, Higher Bourne Farm (prior to 1910, when it was sold), next to the present Chapel, with fields stretching down to the beach. The farmer was Dick Ridler, known to all as Butcher Dick because he was also a butcher in a small way. It is said that he killed only half a bullock a week. The Ordnance Survey map shows Butcher's Plantation just below the village; this was named after Butcher Dick, who owned it.

Not many have a place on a map named after them, but within the last few years a footpath in Porlock has been named Vivien's Way after the Parish Councilor Vivien Perkins, who fought to keep it open against all opposition.

The story is told of two elderly ladies from Doverhay who went on a bus to Minehead for their first ever visit to the cinema. It was a cowboy film, and to them it must have been very realistic. As they came out, one said to the other, 'Caw, coon't 'ee smell the gunpowder.'

Two charabancs on the bridge for an outing to Windsor, c1920.

A West Luccombe man shopping in Minehead went into Hawkins's the chemist's for some rat poison. The chemist asked, 'Rodin?' (a brand of rat poison). 'No,' said the man, 'I missed the bus and walked all the way.'

When Mr Hadley was teaching at Porlock School, one of His Majesty's Inspectors arrived during a Scripture lesson. They had been reading the story of the Good Samaritan. The Inspector asked if one of the boys could repeat the story to him. Keen for a good impression to be made, Mr Hadley asked Donald, who attended Sunday School regularly and would certainly know the story well. Donald retold the story of how the man fell among thieves on his journey from Jerusalem to Jericho, and how both a Priest and a Levite passed him by. Then, he said, the Samaritan came along and picked him up and sat him on his ass. At this the whole class burst out laughing, and there was uproar. I didn't find out what the Inspector had to say.

Local foibles and sayings often come out in conversation without thought; it doesn't mean that anyone using them is ignorant, and they aren't confined to the older generation. Only recently I was talking to a young friend, who told me he had sold his saw bench after advertising it. I asked if he had sold it to someone local. 'No,' he said. 'A chap came from Minehead for it.' When we realised what he had said, we both roared with laughter.

20

THE SECOND WORLD WAR

IN 1939, when war was imminent, all the villagers were fitted with gas masks at the Village Hall. These were carried over the shoulder and, as they were in cardboard boxes, they were usually put into a canvas cover. Schoolchildren had to carry them to school every day.

As the Village Hall was our main building, and used for civil defence, it was protected by sandbags. Lorry loads of sand were brought from Minehead and tipped into the roadway. Gangs of volunteers filled the bags, which were placed around the walls of the Hall.

In the early evening of September 1st the first evacuees arrived from West Ham, having been brought to Minehead by train, then on to Porlock by bus. Mrs Rawles, the Postmaster's wife, was in charge of billeting. After being given tea, the children were sent out with their teachers to various houses in the village, some to live with families, some in a community at Glen Lodge. Later on mothers with babies also arrived, and elderly women. Some wealthier people came privately and rented accommodation. This influx of people made a great difference. The village children, most of whom had never been to London, or even further than Bristol, soon made friends with the West Ham children and quickly picked up London speech and sayings. And it wasn't long before the Londoners were imitating our broad dialect, which was much more noticeable in 1939 than at the present time.

War was declared on Sunday 3rd September 1939 at 11 am, and after the first bombing of Bristol more evacuees arrived. A tea company, Dickson Anderson of Cannon Street, London, had offices in part of The Laurels (now Abbeyfield). The CHA Doverhay Place was taken for a children's nursery, as were Holnicote House and Ashley Coombe House. The village school was packed to capacity, and the Methodist Hall and the Victoria Rooms were used for extra classes. Older boys repaired shoes for the children in the TocH room, which was then next to Burley in Parson Street. It had been taken over and converted into a meeting place by TocH members in 1937. It was formerly a bakery, and then a painter's store.

A collection of waste paper and metal was started. Volunteers stored and sorted paper in a stable belonging to Mr Cape throughout the war. Old iron was dumped at the Tannery in the early days. A special request was made for aluminium, and householders gave whatever saucepans they could spare. They were collected at the shop opposite the Royal Oak, which soon became full.

All buildings had to be blacked out, which caused considerable work, especially as large buildings and shop windows had to have either dark curtains or shutters which could be put up as darkness came. The few street lights had shields over them; cars and even bicycles had to use shielded lights, and pedestrians used torches with paper over the glass, with only a small hole for the light. Some windows high up in the Church and Chapel were permanently blacked out with thick brown paper.

Air Raid Wardens were appointed, and Special Police enrolled, some full-time. The Observer Corps was formed and several men manned the observation post in Sparkhayes Lane in shifts, day and night, between their normal jobs. All aircraft movements were recorded, the post having a direct telephone communication with the Observer Corps at Yeovil. Other observer posts were at Exford and Dunster.

In a radio announcement on 14th May 1940, Secretary of State for War Anthony Eden stated that a Local Defence Volunteer force was to be formed which men not in the Army could join. The first Porlock man to volunteer was a baker's roundsman who had only partial use of one of his arms. He reported to Mr Curtis, the local policeman, who had not yet heard about the force. The LDV was set up, and the men began to train during the evenings and on Sunday mornings. All members wore armbands with the initials 'LDV' (the local lads quickly referred to them as the 'Look, Duck and Vanish' brigade). Some members took their shotguns along as no rifles were yet available. Eventually equipment began to arrive, as well as uniforms. The officers were mainly elderly retired officers from the First World War.

The LDV became the Home Guard and they manned a lookout on Porlock Hill. When not on duty they slept in a hut at Pitt Coombe Head. Invasion was expected at any time, but the men had very little means of defence.

*One of the many pillboxes built in 1940 along the pebble ridge.
This one is at Bossington.*

The pillbox at Porlock Weir.

One man owned a motorbike, so he was the dispatch rider. Porlock platoon was also lucky in that one of its members, Henri Webb, owned a large, fast four-and-a-half-litre Lagonda. Porlock could boast of being a very fast mobile unit that could travel up the straight past Holmbush to Whitstones at eighty miles an hour! Although training continued throughout the war, the Home Guard were fortunately never needed for action, though tragically Mr Farmer, one of the Selworthy members, was accidently shot and killed whilst demonstrating a Sten gun. Their ammunition dump was in the commanding officer's garden in Doverhay; the stores were at Holnicote Stables, and later at the building where Miles's tea offices are now. The firing range for practice was in Granny's Ride.

As part of the defence of our coast, thousands of pill boxes were built, and miles of barbed wire coils were stretched along the top of the beach. Pill boxes were also placed at strategic points commanding roads. Poles about seven foot high covered some larger fields, and piles of stones were heaped on the marsh to discourage or wreck aircraft or gliders if they attempted to land.

To keep watch on shipping activities there were Coast Guards who manned the lookout at Hurlestone Point continuously. There were also two special Coast Guards who, in addition to their daily jobs, patrolled the beach to look for anything washed ashore, including unexploded mines. Mr Jack Marley patrolled each day from Hurlestone to Porlock Weir, and Mr Ewart Perkins from Porlock Weir to Embelle Wood Beach.

The Army moved into Porlock in 1940, after the Dunkirk evacuation. The 58th Company of Royal Engineers drove down from Barton Stacey and were billeted in the Tannery. Officers and NCOs had billets at Frazers and the Cottage Guesthouse. They specialised in chemical warfare. It was thought that perhaps the Germans would use gas, as they had in the 1914-18 war. The REs trained on Exmoor and experimented with the firing of gas shells from rocket launchers mounted on the backs of lorries. On one occasion a couple of live shells were fired by accident.

The Royal Engineers stayed for over a year until they were sent to India. Several married local girls, and returned to live in Porlock after the war.

ENSA concert parties used to come to entertain the troops and civilians in the Village Hall. The troops also had their own concerts and held dances with their own bands. Special days were set aside for fundraising for weapons, perhaps to help buy a warship or a Spitfire. Children helped by organising concerts, and adults would perhaps arrange some other special event.

Occasional training manoeuvres were held on Exmoor, and sometimes the Methodist Hall was used for soldiers to sleep in. So many came that there was almost a continuous flow of traffic through the village. Miles of field telephone cable was laid temporarily along the roads during these operations. Much of Exmoor was a firing range for guns and mortars. There was a tank firing range in the area between Bossington Hill and North Hill, Minehead – North Hill had been used occasionally as a training ground from 1890. Civilians were totally excluded from many of these areas; in some places a red flag was flown during firing practice. Dummy tanks on rails ran along parts of Selworthy Hill and were used as targets. One of these going to and fro could be seen from Porlock.

We must not forget the ladies' part in the war effort: the volunteers who ran a canteen for the troops at Greenaleigh Dairy, now Tesco's, and those who formed the VAD and Red Cross, and trained in nursing and first aid. The Porlock Red Cross was formed at the time of the First World War, when several members worked at Minehead Hospital for wounded soldiers. Land Army girls were billeted in the village and worked with the men on forestry work, and on farms.

Girls also took over the local roundsmen's jobs for the first time because most of the younger men had already gone to the services. Some were away for as long as six years and served in every part of the world. Thirteen lost their lives, and several spent a long time as prisoners of war.

Fire-fighting and first-aid lectures were regularly held, attended by the Red Cross, ARP and Boy Scouts. An Air Training Corps for boys met in the Old Mill in Hawkcombe. The Army Cadets and the Red Cross shared a hut at High Bank, near Splat Barn.

Those of us who were children at the time have many memories. I think we all felt confident of final victory, and didn't worry, perhaps, as much as the adults. We were always interested in the military activities, and took it for granted that guards with fixed bayonets should be posted at the entrance to the Tanyard, then the Army barracks, and that Army lorries were kept under guard in the rickyard at Court Place Farm and at Glen Lodge stables in Hawkcombe. The vehicles were maintained by Army personnel and civilian mechanics at the Central Garage. At Pollard's West End Garage the workshops were converted to make parts for outboard engines for military motor boats.

There were few private cars; most were laid up. Only people with essential needs such as doctors, farmers and traders were allowed petrol. Civilians seldom went beyond Minehead. If a vehicle had to be left unattended, especially at night, the rotor arm would be removed: this was important in case of invasion. This all seems incredible now, but everything was taken very seriously as we saw other countries in Europe gradually taken over by Hitler and the Nazis.

As the war progressed the USA came into it, and it wasn't long before we had American GIs stationed at the Tannery, after the Royal Engineers had left. They drove everywhere in their jeeps and four-wheel drive vehicles. They also used small Piper Cub aeroplanes that landed in Long Back, the largest field on Court Place Farm. The American Army had a very accurate gun on Bossington Hill which fired at a target in the sea off Glenthorne. One Sunday morning, during service time, the whine of a shell was heard as it passed over the village. It fell in a field just in front of the first cottages in West Porlock, much to the consternation of the Army, who came tearing down in their jeeps. Fortunately there was no damage to life or property.

At Stenthill, near Yearnor Farm, the RAF had a small detachment who never talked about their work. After the war we heard that they had been in communication with Cardiff, and used radar to detect enemy planes. We had suspected at the time that this was the work of the unit. Later a radar station was built near East Myne.

The noise of aircraft training was heard every day, especially in good weather. Several airfields were opened in Somerset and Devon, many of which have now reverted to farmland, though others are still in use; Bristol Airport was formerly RAF Lulsgate, whereas Weston Zoyland is no longer used and Merryfield at Ilton is used by the RNAS from Yeovilton.

Although Porlock escaped the bombs, the bombing of Swansea could be clearly seen at night. Planes travelling to and fro could be heard. There was a searchlight battery of troops stationed near Culbone Stables, and another at Webber's Post. A few bombs dropped beside the Dunkery Road, and near Nutscale, leaving huge craters. I remember one night a plane flew very low over the roofs and I jumped out of bed and lay on the floor. The next morning we heard that the soldiers at Webber's Post had fired on it with their rifles.

Several aircraft came down in the valley. The crash landing of the German JU88 is described in the next chapter.

There was also great excitement when, despite the tall posts, a Wellington Bomber made a forced landing in Long Back on 22nd February 1942. When the plane was repaired they knocked down three hedges ready for take-off. A test pilot, an RAF Flight Sergeant, came from Filton to fly it off. The plane started from near the Weir road, by the pound, and taxied down across the fields, but it stopped again near the bottom by Coy Barn. That was the trial run! It taxied back and turned for a new attempt with nearly half the village looking on. Several men and boys were asked to hang on to the tail plane, then the pilot revved up the engines to power, the men let go and the plane taxied fast down over the fields again. Suddenly up came the tail, and then the plane lifted off; skimming over the reed bed, it just cleared the beach and banked to turn up-Channel to make its way back to Weybridge.

During the afternoon of 26th July 1941, while there were children playing in the Recreation Ground, a Spitfire flew over low, lowered its wheels, and flew back and forth about three times. No one realised that the pilot wanted to land. Finally it flew down towards the sea and made a forced landing in a cornfield. Two boys ran up and the pilot asked them where the Post Office was so that he could make a phone call. They directed him up Pound Lane to the village. Crashed aircraft were often transported back through the village on sixty-foot-long articulators.

One very bad crash occurred at Ashley Coombe on a foggy morning, 11th June 1943. A British Halifax four-engined bomber came in from the sea, crashed into the woods and caught fire. Men working in the woods and at the sawmill in Worthy Coombe ran to help. Three men, H. Pollard, T. Cook, and J. Ridler, tried to get the airmen out but there was an explosion and Jack Ridler of Porlock Weir was so severely burned he had to spend some time in hospital. At that time Ashley Coombe House was used as a children's nursery by Dr Barnardo's. The plane had skimmed past the windows at the back of the house, missing it literally by inches. Had it hit the house, there would have been an even bigger tragedy. As it was, four of the crew were killed and two injured. The scar up over the woods remained for a very long time. A memorial to the dead was later erected in the wood.

Often convoys of ships were seen out at sea, bringing supplies from America. One morning I went over to the butcher's shop near the school and happened to look out to sea. I saw a large ship sailing down the Channel. Suddenly, and very quickly, her bows went up into the air and she sank stern first. It all happened in a few moments, probably the result of a mine or U-boat attack. U-boats operated in the Channel, and parachute mines were dropped by German aircraft (two Minehead boatmen were killed by one of these mines). The beach became thick with huge lumps of oil, which stayed until it dispersed naturally.

There was great excitement one day earlier on, in 1940, when the roads were covered in ice. That year there was a terrible winter. There were no snow ploughs then, so all the vehicles had chains on their wheels. We saw a huge column of smoke coming up from the west. Everyone rushed towards the school so that they could see what was happening. An oil tanker was alight from stem to stern, the flames rising several hundred feet and the smoke to about a thousand feet into the air. Planes were flying through the smoke, but it was obvious that no one could be saved. This was one more ship with a vital supply of aviation spirit lost. Later, after the war, we learnt that she had been sunk by a German U33 submarine.

At the beginning of the war the government introduced rationing of foodstuffs. Prices rose, but everyone was allowed their ration, unlike in the First World War when the poor suffered badly. A scheme was devised by Williton RDC for producing meat pies, which were made by Burgess's and Stenner's at Porlock and sold by the Women's Institute.

Prior to D-day the build-up of troops and aircraft increased. Training was stepped up and we saw many gliders being towed by aeroplanes, as well as large pontoons for the Mulberry Harbour being towed down-Channel by tugs. Because of censorship during the war, very little military activity was reported in the local paper, only the usual items and adverts of interest to the general public. The national daily papers and radio did, however, give a good idea of the progress and setbacks of the war effort, and, as many people attended cinemas, the 'Newsreel' kept us up to date.

Being a country area free from bombing, most people fared well in Porlock, although sadly many families lost loved ones as a result of the war. A memorial to the fallen of the First World War had been erected in 1921: a cross of Doulton stone recorded twenty-four Porlock men killed. After the Second War the plaque was recarved and the lettering made smaller so that thirteen more names could be added.

21

THE GERMAN JUNKERS 88

Shot down on to Porlock Beach during the Battle of Britain on 27th September 1940

AT THE TIME I was a schoolboy attending what was then Minehead County School (it became Minehead Grammar School and is now Minehead Middle School). On that particular morning, a Friday, I was at home in Porlock; having felt unwell, I had stayed in bed. Suddenly I heard planes overhead and people shouting in the street. I jumped out of bed and looked out of the window. A Spitfire flew over, doing the victory roll, as we called it, and people shouted that a German plane was down. Immediately all thought of sickness left me! I pulled on my clothes, left the house and ran through the street with all the others. When I got to the pound at the top of High Bank I joined Miss Doris Ridler of Doverhay Farm, who had arrived at the same time on her bike. Together we ran across Court Place fields, through Long Back to the marshes and on to New Works. We arrived just in time to

The German Junkers 88 on Porlock Beach.

see three German prisoners come over the top of the beach, with several men escorting them.

I well remember how they were dressed (they were wearing forage caps), and that one was a very tall man. There was great excitement. I can remember old Farmer Dave Ridler saying, 'They've got 'em!' It was said later that he was waving a pitchfork but, as this was quite a common farm implement to be carrying in those days, it didn't register with me.

Most of the spectators were workmen who had been building pill boxes all along the beach (most of which have since been demolished). I think only one Englishman was armed: he was a naval officer who always wore a pistol in a holster. He was in charge of a salvage party who had been working on a Fleet Air Arm plane, a Fairy Albacore, which had a fortnight before made a forced landing on the marsh at Sparkhayes.

The German prisoners walked quietly across the marsh, then they were driven away in Mr Jim Pollard's car, together with PC Curtis. Escorted by Mr Bert Rice on his pony, they were taken to Porlock and then to Minehead Police Station. The rear gunner, Corporal Wilhelm Reuhl, had been killed. His body was brought out later; covered with a blanket, it lay at the top of the beach. He was buried in Porlock Cemetery. The prisoners were interned in a POW camp in Canada for the rest of the war.

With many others, I went to the top of the beach where we could see the plane lying at low water mark, near Redsands. It was a JU 88, a fighter bomber capable of a speed exceeding 300 mph (fast for those days). It carried a crew of four and was armed with three hand-held machine guns. No one approached the plane because we were told there were unexploded bombs aboard. An Army guard was soon on the scene, and of course the tide soon came up over the plane.

On Saturday and Sunday sightseers came from miles around and took away parts of the plane as souvenirs. The machine guns were given to Minehead School Air Training Corps.

The plane had been chased from the Bristol area by three Spitfires and they were shooting as it flew over Minehead. My friends at school had also had an exciting time as it flew over the school. Ignoring their Air Raid Drill, they all rushed out on to the verandahs and the masters had to shout at them to come back. The plane then flew very low down the Porlock Vale, smoke pouring from one engine. Mr Ernie Pollard of Porlock Weir was feeding his chickens when he saw the planes

approaching. The Junkers flew over the beach, out to sea, and then turned shorewards and made a perfect landing in shallow water.

Two of the Spitfires had returned. The final credit went to Pilot Officer Eric Mars of 152 Squadron. He later lost his life: he was shot down over Brest in 1941.

After a few days the German plane was washed up by the high tides to the top of the beach. I well remember this as, whilst playing on the plane I slid off the slippery wing and fell into the sea. I had to walk home completely soaked.

Andy Hyde of Minehead was a Sergeant in the School Air Training Corps and he was responsible for cleaning and renovating the machine guns from the Junkers. He told me that the guns were Rheinmetal Borsig, and that the boys had been given not only the guns but also some ammunition. Like true schoolboys, he and his pals fired a gun from his bedroom window. There are still marks of the tracer bullets on the chimney of the house in Minehead.

The plane had been carrying highly sophisticated photographic equipment in order to photograph the dock gates of the Manchester Ship Canal. Those were days when people were dedicated to total war, and yet the prisoners were treated kindly, and the dead man's grave was respected.

The pilot, Helmut Ackenhauser, the tall man I had noticed, has since returned to visit Minehead Police Station, where he had his photograph taken in the cell he occupied in 1940. He also met Mr Eddie Jones who has tended the grave of the rear gunner. The family of Wilhelm Reuhl who, we have been told, was barely eighteen years old, have also visited the grave, one of the best kept in the cemetery. Later I met Wilhelm Reuhl's brother whilst he was on a visit from Germany. He was eight years old when his brother was killed.

22

THE LIBERATOR MONUMENT

MANY PEOPLE ask about the monument on Porlock Marsh. This is to the memory of the brave United States airmen whose plane crashed in the marsh on 29th October 1942. Our American allies were then operating in England. The plane was a long-range bomber, transport and reconnaissance aircraft, a Consolidated B-24 D Liberator with four 1,200 hp radial engines, a wingspan of 110 feet, a length of 67 feet 2 inches, a maximum speed of 300 mph at 30,000 feet and a range of 2,100 miles. It carried a crew of twelve and had ten .50 machine guns. More than 18,000 B-24 planes were built and served the USAAF, the RAF and the Commonwealth Air Forces in every theatre of war.

This particular plane, which was helping RAF Coastal Command, took off from Holmsley, South Hampshire at 7.20 am on 29th October to fly on anti-submarine patrol in the Bay of Biscay. When it was returning at about 3.30 pm it was seen by two boys, Alan Perkins and Brian Richards, to hit a point near the top of Bossington Hill and swing round. Pieces fell off: a wheel and part of the undercarriage landed at the bottom of Sparkhayes Lane, and the rest of the plane crashed on to the marsh. The weather was dreadful: it was a very wet day with low cloud all around. Amongst the first on the scene were Mr Cecil Westcott, Nurse Bragg, the District Nurse, and members of the Observer Corps. Mr Westcott carried the nurse through the swamp to the plane, but little could be done. Only one man, S/Sgt H.B. Thorpe, was still alive. Very little of the plane was seen by local people as its remains were salvaged within a few days.

The simple monument on Porlock Marsh was erected by members of the Porlock Branch of the British Legion, made of materials available at that time. It has been moved from its original site so that now more people are able to see it. A later plaque was put on the monument, paid for by the widows of the airmen who died in the crash.

The plane belonged to the 330th Bomb Squadron of 93rd Bomb

Group (Heavy), whose main base was at Hardwick, near Norwich in Norfolk. Because of their many movements, the Squadron was known as Ted's Travelling Circus, Ted being Colonel Ted Timberlake, the Group Commanding Officer. On 25th May 1987 an impressive Memorial Stone was dedicated to the men of the 93rd near the village of Topcroft, at the North Eastern corner of the airfield site. The crew are buried at the American Military Cemetery in Cambridge. The one 'unknown' on the Memorial was Sgt S.C. Prekel.

23

CHANGING LIFESTYLES

THE AVERAGE READER is probably most interested in changes that have taken place during the last 150 to 200 years. If we take Porlock in, say, 1869, we find a small community still fairly self-supporting, a small sea port at Porlock Weir and a market town ruled by the Vestry, who appointed two overseers of the poor and two waywardens. It was mainly an agricultural area, but the village satisfied most of its own needs, producing footwear, clothing, carts and tools. It also had the Tannery. Village life revolved around the Church. The Rector, the Rev Sylvanus Brown, also used to referee boxing matches on the bridge. Boxing had replaced the formerly vicious sport of wrestling, which used to allow contestants to wear iron-shod boots so that they could kick their opponents' shins the harder, to knock them off balance. The Old Chapel, which had opened in 1837, was also very active.

Regarding transport, the railway had reached Watchet in 1862, the first Stage Coach had arrived in 1843, and there was a carrier into the village every Friday.

The Penny Post had started in 1840. Letters arrived at 8.55 am and were collected at 5.30 pm.

There were the Old and New Clubs (forerunners of Friendly Societies). The Old Club dated back to 1776 and the New Club to 1819. They were organised for helping one another in times of sickness and distress, and with the cost of funerals. There were later the C of E Temperance Society, the Band of Hope and the Rachobites. For leisure there was the 'Club Day' – which sometimes lasted three or four days!

The Minehead and Dunster Village Hospital was opened at Dunster in 1867. There were also the village charities, which survive in an amalgamated form.

There was no compulsory education, but a small school had been opened in Parson Street (where the schoolmaster was paid £32 a year) and there was a dame-school at Porlock Weir.

Wages were between six and seven shillings per week, but the cost of food was comparable: for example, a pound of sugar cost 3d, a pound of cheese 9d, a pound of tea 2/6, a cwt of coal 8½d, beefsteak 7¼d a pound and chops 2¾d a pound.

Most of the houses were thatched, and many had cob walls. Many of these have now either disappeared or been extensively modernised. R.D. Blackmore

Porlock Band, 1875.

A cricket match at the Recreation Ground, c1950, before the houses at Crawter Drive or Hawkcombe View were built.

published his book *Lorna Doone* in 1869; he termed it 'A Romance of Exmoor'. Much of the background was obtained in Porlock, from interviews with local people.

In 1855 a new dock had been built at the Weir. There was only one hotel, the Anchor, at Porlock Weir. And in the 1870s we still had a Lord of the Manor, Colonel Blathwayt.

During 1871 many children died, their deaths brought on by drinking water from the open stream. Sanitation was very bad because there was no mains drainage.

In 1872 the Rev Walter Hook was appointed Rector of Porlock. The Church rate was abolished in 1874. Then in 1876 the first water rate was charged.

In 1876, too, a branch of the Ancient Order of Foresters was formed, and it was very strong for many years. The same year the New School was opened. A brass band had been started the previous year, and attended local functions.

The first cricket was played in 1865. The cricket field was first mentioned in 1877: this was on Glebe land and was later to become our present Recreation Ground.

The main diet of the villagers was fish and potatoes. The oyster beds were being fished from 1870 and, although oysters were sent to Bristol, plenty must have been eaten locally as many shells have been found in village gardens.

Carriages (possibly for a wedding reception at the Lorna Doone Hotel) outside Tom Smith's saddler's shop, c1910. Note the workers in their aprons.

Parish. This was unfortunate for Porlock folk because they had to pay for burial, whereas Luccombe parishioners were buried free. In 1894 the first Council Elections were held, and a high poll was reported.

The village was beginning to be known as a centre for hunting and for tourism. By 1894 there were coaches to Minehead three times a week in winter, and daily in summer months.

Also in 1894 a Lending Library was started with three hundred volumes, so it can be assumed the villagers were not so backward as in other parts of Britain. The Library continued in Dovery Manor,

The Markets stopped between 1880 and 1890. In 1889 the first district nurse was appointed. We find that tea was very expensive, and this encouraged people to drink more beer.

Rugby football was played in 1882, but in 1887 soccer started. The transition to the new game must have been difficult as the press reported that in one of the early football matches 'one of the Porlock team picked up the ball and ran'.

In 1891 the Church was extensively restored, and in the same year the new cemetery was opened in Hawkcombe on land actually belonging to Luccombe

The Lorna Doone Hotel and Royal Oak, 2009.

which had been restored by Sir Charles Chadwyck-Healey, and was run by volunteers up to 1969. The building also housed the Reading Room from 1899, and it continues as a Billiard and Snooker Club, with a Museum. There has been a major restoration of the building with a grant from the Heritage Lottery Fund and others. The restored building was officially opened on Saturday 9th May 2009.

In 1893 there was a great change when up to

The old Castle Inn., now the Castle Hotel.

a dozen cottages which surrounded the Churchyard were demolished in order to widen Parson Street.

In 1897, at the time of Queen Victoria's Diamond Jubilee, the Victoria Rooms were opened. The top room was used for Church meetings and the bottom room was a Reading Room for village men. The work cost £250.

About this time, 1886, the Three Horse Shoes Inn was closed and sold for £600, and a new hotel, the Lorna Doone Hotel, was built on the site. The old Castle Inn was sold in 1887 for £900 and rebuilt as the Castle Hotel in 1890.

Porlock could perhaps have been very different had the railway proposed in 1885 from Porlock Weir to

Hawcombe Water Mill, c1920.

The Dogs of Devon (1935), *Hia-watha* (1936) and a performance of Handel's *Messiah*. The first concerts were held in the School, but in 1925 the Village Hall was opened. The Parson Street Reading Room put on a popular concert each year.

Since then many village events have been held: whist drives, dances and the annual Horticultural Shows. There have been local shows: *The Smugglers* and a sequel to *Lorna Doone*, with the music and lyrics by local young people, produced by the Guides and Scouts. These were followed in more recent years by panto-mimes, mainly local productions of the old favourites. In the winter months parties for children and older folk organised by the British Legion, TocH and the Women's Institute were eagerly looked forward to.

Another annual event, enjoyed by young and old alike, was the visit of the circus, Sangers, Robert Fossett or Bertram Mills, with their horses, lions and elephants. These used to be a great attraction for the village.

Carnivals have been resumed in recent years, starting with the 1969 Lorna Doone Centenary events. It was whilst watching this carnival that someone was heard to remark how good it was for Porlock's first carnival. An eighty-year-old standing near me said,

Minehead, and that proposed in 1898 from Minehead to Lynmouth, materialised – although I suspect that Dr Beeching would have closed it in the 1950s as uneconomical! This project had been on the cards for a number of years, as was Mr Knight's proposed railway to bring iron ore from Simonsbath to Porlock Weir, another enterprise which failed.

This brings us to 1900, when the first motor car climbed Porlock Hill, thus starting a new era for Porlock. Wages had risen to 10/- per week, 9/- for a farm labourer. It was still a long day's work at the Tannery. The hours were from 6am to 6pm, finishing at 4pm on Saturdays and with no work on Sundays. Electricity came in 1911. The Porlock Electric Company was formed, and electricity was produced by the Water Mill in Hawkcombe.

Porlock has always been a sociable place with its clubs and societies. As far back as 1903 the Porlock Choral Society had a fine choir, whose performances included *Merry Old England* (1903), *The King of Sherwood* (1908), *Ali Baba and the Forty Black Sheep* (1909), *The Mandarin* (1910),

'I can remember carnivals when I was a boy in Porlock.' Nothing is new!

From 1900 onwards life had been improving in the village, although things changed quite slowly. Except for the people who had moved here and built homes, the working people, farmers and shopkeepers were in the main from families who had lived in the area for generations. After 1900 the motor car was occasionally to be seen, in the summer time in particular. Shops were growing in number and the roads were improving, although the main street wasn't tarred until after

Outing to Cheddar Caves in the early 1900s.

Lady Mary, Countess of Lovelace (on the right) after the stone-laying ceremony
at the Village Hall. The hall was opened in 1925.
The architect was C.F. Annesley Voisey.

the First World War. The dust in summer was kept down by Mr Ridler of Doverhay Farm with a water cart, at the cost of 3/- per day. Because Mr Ridler was paid by Porlock Parish Council, he didn't water the Doverhay side of the main street, which was in Luccombe Parish.

At the beginning of the 20th century there was a horse bus service to Minehead. Then in the 1920s a service was started by the Minehead and Porlock-Porlock Weir Blue Motor Company which did sterling service up to the late 1950s. In the 1930s the Mascot Company ran a service which was taken over

Porlock Scouts, 1910.

by the Western National, later Southern National and Scarlet Coaches, and now Quantock Coaches, which include double-deckers.

If anyone was ill, the hospital was now at Minehead, the Dunster Cottage Hospital having closed. There was also a large Isolation Hospital built at Venniford (now private dwellings). Isolation cases were first admitted into a temporary hospital at Tivington.

Most of the men worked in the village. Some children attended the new Secondary School at Minehead after 1929. The place of assembly in the village was the bridge, where a crowd of men would gather during the dinner hour. They would wait until a few minutes before 2 pm before dispersing to their various places of employment.

As well as the Village Hall, which was opened in 1925 by the Countess of Lovelace, the Recreation Ground, which was gradually enlarged, served the village for many activities.

The Churches continued their work, serving old and young alike, with Sunday Worship, the Sunday School and Youth Clubs.

Early in the century, when young women went out to service they often married the local village men. Life in Porlock carried on peacefully, except of course for the interruption of two world wars. It was due to these events that there was more movement of the population, and many men afterwards brought home wives from places far away from Porlock.

The Boy Scouts were formed in Porlock as early as 1909 by Mr Salaman, the owner of Doverhay Place. They could boast a drum and bugle band in those days. The Scouts have continued, although with a few breaks, until today. Guiding was started in Porlock after the First World War by Miss Holmes, the Rector's daughter, and was later followed by the Cubs and Brownies. All have had their ups and downs, as have the Youth Clubs.

Even with the coming of cars, horse riding for pleasure has remained popular, and there have always been hacks and hunters for hire. Mr Joe Collins came in the 1920s from Exeter and started the Riding Stables which later took over the Tannery, where he first started the Porlock Vale Riding School. He was succeeded by his son Tony, who was very well known in the equestrian world. He trained the British Olympic Team at Porlock in 1952 for the Olympic Games in Helsinki. Unfortunately he lost his life in an aeroplane crash in the Mediterranean. Polo was also popular, and games were played in a field at Newbridge.

After the Second World War the tourist boom came, and a great bed-and-breakfast trade was done by some of the villagers. Nearly everyone arrived by train at Minehead, and came on by bus to Porlock. As the motor car began to appear again after the war, the private bed-and-breakfast trade declined. The trend in holidays was changing and visitors were more likely to go to hotels and guest houses.

Camping was also becoming more popular as better equipment became available. Before the war large camps of Scouts, Guides and other groups were dotted around the farms during the summer, but they are now confined mainly to the campsite at Horner.

Early in the 20th century families used to go off to pick 'worts' (whortleberries) during the school summer holidays. This was a source of income for poorer people, who often used the extra money to buy clothes. In 1938 worts were offered to dealers at 4d per quart (they were always measured in a quart measure) after the leaves had been fanned out with a tea tray as the worts were dropped on to a sheet. When the war came the price rose to 2/- to 2/6 a quart. Mr Cecil Westcott, the Porlock fruiterer, used to buy worts and collect them from pickers on Exmoor. The fruit was then taken to Minehead Station and sent to London and cities in the Midlands. Most were for human consumption, although a blue dye could be made from them. The largest amount sent by Mr Westcott by train was an incredible one ton, all packed in small punnets! After the war, with higher wages, wort-picking declined and many of the favourite hills were converted to pasture.

Now the only people picking the fruit tend to be visitors who stop their cars and take some home to make whortleberry tart to eat with cream. But even the cream is now unobtainable from the farms, so we can see how life has changed dramatically over the last century.

Social changes have brought greater mobility of labour. Consequently fewer people spend their entire lives in one place. But many people now retire here.

In previous days, people's lives were centred on one community. Life and death were celebrated by the whole community because everyone knew everyone else. I am thankful that I grew up in Porlock at a time when it was still a small close-knit community, and with practically free access to a much less intensively farmed Exmoor.

Today there are visitors all the year round. I hope that they will enjoy Porlock and its surroundings, but I also hope that we are able to keep it unspoiled – even though we may have to accept many changes.

Residents of Porlock today can be thankful for many of the changes to its way of life. Life here is good and the surroundings are beautiful. I myself love it. I have no wish to live anywhere else.

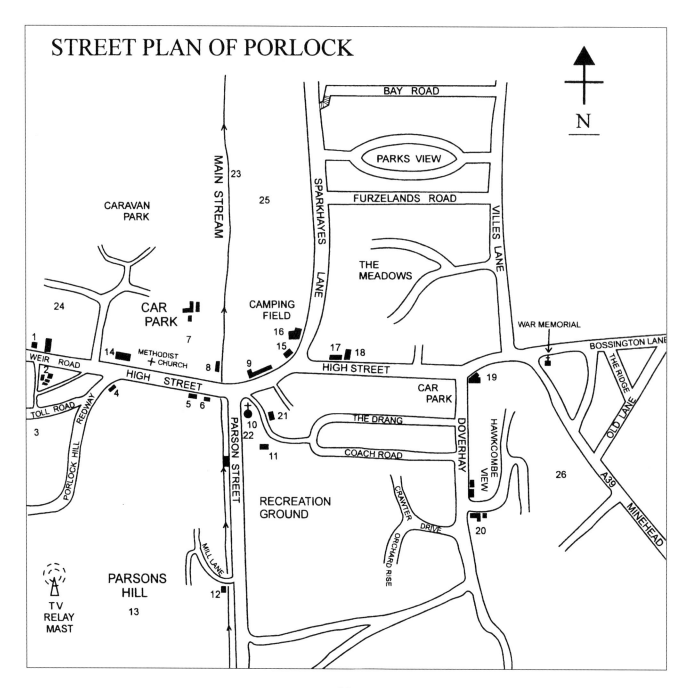

STREET PLAN OF PORLOCK

N

BAY ROAD

PARKS VIEW

FURZELANDS ROAD

MAIN STREAM

23

25

CARAVAN PARK

SPARKHAYES LANE

VILLES LANE

THE MEADOWS

24

CAR PARK

7

CAMPING FIELD

16

15

WAR MEMORIAL

BOSSINGTON LANE

1

14

METHODIST CHURCH

8

17 18

HIGH STREET

THE RIDGE

WEIR ROAD

9

19

CAR PARK

OLD LANE

2

HIGH STREET

5 6

4

REDWAY

TOLL ROAD

3

PORLOCK HILL

PARSON STREET

10

22

21

THE DRANG

COACH ROAD

DOVERHAY

HAWKCOMBE VIEW

26

A39

MINEHEAD

11

RECREATION GROUND

CRAWTER DRIVE

ORCHARD RISE

20

MILL LANE

TV RELAY MAST

PARSONS HILL

13

12

PLACES OF INTEREST IN PORLOCK

1 THE POUND The Pound was used for holding stray animals and has been used within living memory. The present building was erected after 1844, before which the Pound was on the left of the old entrance to Court Place.

SPLAT BARN 'Splat' means allotment, so there is possibly some connection with the manor strip system. The house is marked as a building of historic interest on the six-inch map of 1929.

2 COURT PLACE Court Place is where the Lord of the Manor lived. In 1420 the Manor House had a hall and a great chamber. In 1640 Gerard writes: '…not farre from the Town you may see an Ancient Manor House'. The house was burnt down in the early 19th century and a new one was built on a site nearby. The Manor Court was still being held in 1842.

3 THE PARKS AND CONYGAR The Parks were useful for keeping pigs. Tenants paid 2d for 'wood-weyght' (the right to take wood) and 1d for 'ferneheu' (the right to take ferns). The 'Coney-garth' or Cony Acre was where the Lord of the Manor caught rabbits.

4 SHIP INN In 1797 the Poet Laureate Robert Southey stayed at the Ship Inn and wrote the poem beginning 'Porlock, thy verdant vale…' The coach to Lynmouth stopped there and took on two extra horses, hired from local farmers or traders, to help it climb up Porlock Hill.

5 CASTLE INN Once thatched, the old Castle Inn was sold in 1887 for £900 and then demolished to make way for the present Castle Hotel.

6 TOWN MILL The Manor or Town Mill was sited between Abbeyfield and the Castle Hotel. The twenty customary tenants of 1306 were bound by agreement to clean out the Mill Pond on Hockday (the second Tuesday after Easter). The Bailiffs' Rolls of 1419-26 reveal that Lady Harrington had to spend much money to keep the mill in repair.

7 THE TANNERY Once the home of Porlock's largest industry, the production of leather, the Tanyard is first mentioned in 1794 when it belonged to Abraham Phelps. It closed after the First World War.

8 MARKET PLACE The Market Place was the site of the weekly Market as well as two or three annual Fairs which were first granted in 1366, then again in 1614. Tradition speaks of a 'beautiful market house', but where it was is not known. There was still a Market Cross in Porlock in 1810. The Tithe Map of 1844 shows a small building near the Central Garage, parallel to the river, which is called the Market House. Markets disappeared around 1800 but Fairs continued until the 1870s.

9 ROSE AND CROWN INN Only two inns are mentioned in a directory of 1794: the Ship and the Rose and Crown, where it is believed R.D. Blackmore once stayed. In 1870 the landlady was summoned for rowdy behaviour in the Crown, which was closed down about ten years later.

10 THE CHURCH OF ST DUBRICIUS The earliest part of the Church dates from the 13th century. It is thought to have been rebuilt by Sir Simon Fitz-Roges at the beginning of the 14th century and his effigy still stands in the Church. St Dubricius was a Welsh saint and it seems very likely that West Somerset was Christianised from Wales. The Church was probably built on a site once used for pagan worship.

11 THE OLD RECTORY Part of the Old Rectory dates back to the 15th century or earlier. The first Porlock Rector was John, son of Rogo, appointed in 1297. Since 1559 the living has been in the gift of the Crown. The New Rectory was built in 1992.

12 HAWKCOMBE OR PARSONAGE MILL
This was part of the Rectorial Manor.

13 PARSONS HILL So called because it belonged to the Church Manor, the hill is also sometimes referred to as Burley.

14 THE OLD SCHOOL The Old School, which now houses the Information Centre, the Library, the Council Office and the Lovelace Centre, opened in 1876 and was closed when the present school in Parson Street opened in 1993. An earlier schoolroom was sited in Parson Street and was run by subscription.

15 THE CHAPEL The Old Chapel was built in 1837, nearly thirty years after the first Methodist services were held in the village. The New Chapel opened in 1927 and the original building is now a café.

16 SPARKHAYES Formerly a farm, Sparkhayes was first mentioned in 1383 and once belonged to the Earl of Lovelace.

17 THE THREE HORSE SHOES This building was on the site of the Lorna Doone Hotel and is mentioned in the 1822 Register of Inns.

18 THE ROYAL OAK On the Tithe Map there is an inn next door to the Three Horse Shoes called the Somerset Inn, owned by Abraham Sparks Jnr. This was probably the Royal Oak.

19 DOVERY COURT OR MANOR Now the Museum and Snooker Club, the Court was probably first used as a Dower House for the Lady when her husband died. 'An example of a remarkably small Manor house of the fifteenth century', it was restored in 1894, paid for by Sir Charles E.H. Chadwyck-Healey, and is now owned by Porlock Parish Council.

20 DOVERHAY FARMS AND INNS Both Lower and Higher Doverhay Farms (now no longer worked) were once the homes of substantial yeomen. There were two taverns in Doverhay in 1280, in one of which a man was murdered – the event led to a fine for the entire Hundred of Carhampton.

21 THE PRIEST'S HOUSE / THE HARRINGTON CHANTRY The Harrington Memorial in the Church is one of the finest of its kind and was erected in memory of Lord and Lady Harrinton. The first Priest was appointed in 1476 and the Chantry closed in 1546. The Priest had to reside 'in a certain messuage, hard by the cemetery of the church' and the Chaplains had to provide bread and cheese and ten gallons of good beer, to be eaten and drunk in memory of the Lord and Lady after the anniversary service.

22 HOUSES AROUND THE CHURCH These were knocked down in c1890 and the position of the road was altered. There was an archway into the Church and it was here that the Stocks were kept in the early 19th century. There was a dwelling over the archway and one of the houses was a Malt House (one of six in Porlock in the early 1800s).

23 MESNE STREAM The meadowland, the most valued land in the area, was held in common and bordered the stream.

24 THE BUTTYARD This was where archery was practised by order of the King. The field is now covered with bungalows.

25 THE FIELDS In 1306 twenty villeins held a furlong each, in return for many duties to the Lord of the Manor. The field (i.e. the open field) is frequently mentioned in the Bailiffs' Rolls of 1419-26, but only in connection with haymaking. In 1509 the common fields were called Netherlands, Cowlease, Uppastyle and Pownde Park. There were also Wheatpark, Buttyard, Allerpark and Conygar.

26 DOVERHAY / LUCCOMBE The separation of Doverhay from Porlock goes back at least to Saxon times. The name is possibly British in origin. Doverhay was joined to Porlock Civil Parish in 1928.

27 THE DECOY / COY BARN Cygnets were taken from the Marsh for Lady Harrington's table in 1420 – 'the expenses of divers men taking cygnets by order of the Lady: 10d'.

BIBLIOGRAPY AND SUGGESTED FURTHER READING

Allen, N.V. *Exmoor Place Names.* Alcombe Books.

Bouquet, M. *No Gallant Ship.* H&C, 1959.

Chadwyck-Healey, Sir Charles E.H. *The History of Part of West Somerset.* Sotheran, 1901.

Collinson-Morley. *Porlock, West Porlock, Porlock Weir and Culbone.* Cox.

Corner, Dennis. *The Book of Porlock.* Halsgrove, 1999.

Eeles, F.C. *The Church of St Dubricius, Porlock.* B&P, 1935.

Farr, G. *Somerset Harbours.* Johnson, 1954.

Gillman, J. *Nineteenth-Century West Somerset Sailing Ships.* Unpublished.

Halliday, M. *Description of the Monuments and Effigies in Porlock Church.* Torquay, 1882.

Hawkins, Mac. *Somerset at War, 1939-1945.* Dovecote Press, 1988.

Hook, Rev Walter M.A. *A History of the Ancient Church of Porlock, and of the Patron Saint, St Dubricius and His Times.* Parker, 1893.

Hurley, J. *Exmoor in Wartime, 1939-45.* Exmoor Press, 1978.

Marshall, J.J. *Exmoor Sporting and Otherwise.* E&S, 1948.

Morris, J. (ed). *Doomesday Book (No. 8): Somerset.* Phillimore, 1980.

Page, J.Ll.W. *An Exploration of Exmoor.* Seeley, 1890.

Pointon, A.G. *Methodism in West Somerset.* PP, 1982.

Ridler, J.K. *A Selworthy Notebook.* PP, 1983.

Savage, J. *History of the Hundred of Carhampton.* Strong, 1830.

Smith, G. *Smuggling in the Bristol Channel, 1700-1850.* Countryside Books, 1989.

Symons, W. *Early Methodism in West Somerset.* Kelly, 1895.

Waters, B. *The Bristol Channel.* Dent, 1955.

Whyte-Melville, G.J. *Katerfelto: A Story of Exmoor.* C&H, 1875.

ACKNOWLEDGEMENTS

MY THANKS must go to the many people who, over the years, knowing of my interest in Porlock and its history, have encouraged me to write this book.

To the many local people who have let me talk to them, and have given me valuable inform-ation of their own memories.

To the Porlock Museum Committee, and especially the late W.R. Hadley, who collected so much information, which Mrs J. Hadley has kindly allowed me to use.

To my wife who has spent many hours reading over, and typing from my longhand writing.

The photographs are mainly from my own colour transparencies, and from my collection of old photographs.

Some of the old ones are from the Porlock Museum Collection.

Burgess's baker's shop before enlargement in 1929.